LIVE FORGIVEN

Discovering the Life You Never Thought Possible

Dr. Jeff Warren

Live Forgiven
Discovering the Life You Never Thought Possible
by Dr. Jeff Warren

Printed in the United States of America

ISBN 978-1-60647-486-0

www.xulonpress.com

To Whitney … your constant joy and persevering spirit motivate me.

To Emily … your passion for life and tender heart for the hurting and forgotten move me.

To Travis, my "best pal buddy" … your clever humor and endless creativity inspire me.

Without the three of you I would not know this explosion of joy, laughter, and adventure that is life in our family every single day. I love being your dad.

To Stacy, my enchanting wife … without you I would not know the pleasure of partnering through this life with my best friend, constant encourager, and selfless companion. I love you with all my heart. I'm so grateful we're on this journey together.

To Jesus … without You there is no freedom to live forgiven.

Table of Contents

Acknowledgements

In his book *Leadership is an Art*, Max Depree writes, "The first task of a leader is to define reality. The last is to say 'thank you'. In between the two, the leader is a servant and a debtor. That sums up the artful leader."[1] I spend most of my time seeking to "define reality" for myself and others. I am acutely aware that I am indebted to anyone who would allow me to lead and in this case, anyone who would read this book. So, even before you begin, "Thank you."

Every book has a story before the story and most of this book is *my* story to this point. In the end, our lives are the converging stories of people in it and mine has been marked by some amazing people of influence. I am first indebted to my church family. The people of First Baptist Church, McKinney, Texas are the most loving, sacrificial, and willing servants I've ever known. My family *loves* serving with you. Thank you for allowing us to be, not only "normal," but for encouraging us to put our family first. Doing life with such a grace-filled and Christ-centered people is the joy of my life.

I'm blessed with more friends than anyone on the planet and I'm indebted to more than I can name. As I think of the key influencers on my journey, one is Dan Sleet, my lifelong friend who is still "closer than a brother." Together we forged a trajectory of life like the well-worn path to our childhood homes. My friend, Jonathan Scott, is a constant source of inspiration. Every time we talk I'm challenged to think deeper about our God and who He really is. I'm indebted to countless members of FBC Charlotte who helped lay the spiritual foundation of my life. I'm grateful for the influence of Young Life and Campus Crusade during my most formative years of high school and college. My friends at Park Cities Baptist Church have forever shaped my life and my family. It was while serving with you in Dallas that much of the content of this book was formed in my heart and birthed into my life.

The title of this book came from a single moment of inspiration with my friend, Mike Abernathy. Thanks, Mike, for bringing my life's message down to two words. I'm forever indebted to my precious friend and spiritual mentor, Jack Jernigan, who went Home to the Lord during the writing of this book. He was a constant source of encouragement and inspiration as a writer himself. To countless others who have believed in me to help make this project possible, you know who you are. Guys like Dano, J.P., Nuge, Pat, Jerry, Mark, Greg, Ben, Matt, and the team at Pursuant. Thanks to my accountability partner and colleague, Chris Stull, our entire Executive Team, and ministerial staff. I am forever indebted to the entire staff at FBC McKinney. This apostolic covenant that we've entered into is a rare and costly gift. You have not only been fellow pioneers in this missional adventure, but have encouraged my thought and life throughout this project. What a ride it has been through these incredible days!

Biggest thanks go to Nora LaPrade, my ministry assistant, for her ongoing investment in my life, family, and ministry. She is truly a partner in ministry and has served as chief editor for this book. Nora, I enjoy working with you every day. Thank you to Julie Brants and my wife, Stacy, who did a great job on the final editing.

My dad and my mom, Gene and Louise Warren, continue to be amazing parents and have been the most influential people in my life. My brothers, Dan and Kevin, have always believed in me and continue to love and encourage me. My in-laws, Freeman and Billie Smith, are a constant source of support and encouragement. Choosing to marry your daughter was one of the few moments of true genius I've ever had.

Finally, I want to acknowledge my family. I'm indebted to my children; Whitney, Emily, and Travis for allowing me the greatest privilege of being your dad. Of all the roles I play in life, that's the one I cherish the most. I absolutely love being your dad. Stacy has once again been my primary encourager and anything of value that I've brought to this project can be traced back to her. She is an amazing mom and an even better wife.

Introduction

"Jesus is an evil person to me."

If words had physical force I suppose I would have been on the ground. I had not heard anything quite like that. Jesus was at least "kind," even "cool," but not "evil." Even more amazing was that she really meant it. She didn't say it for a kind of shock value or to challenge me. She meant it. She believed it. Of course, I knew there was a long, painful story behind her opinion. I could tell by looking at her that there was a story.

I was in Nigeria, West Africa, speaking to hundreds of teenagers at an international school. Many of them were Muslims, others Europeans or expatriates, and some were "MK's" (aka missionary kids). She was among the latter. Her parents were missionaries in Africa serving the Lord while she lived in a hostel which was really just a house for some of the missionary kids at the school while their parents were out on the field. I met "Samantha" (not her real name) earlier in the week. She wore very thick, dark eyeliner, and her bleached-blond hair hung over her face as if trying to hide something or someone.

I had been given the daunting task of keeping the attention of mostly disinterested and skeptical students who entered reluctantly into yet another "Spiritual Emphasis Week," a yearly event designed to expose the students to the claims of Jesus Christ. I think it ranked just above algebra, but below political science, as the most exciting way to spend a couple of hours during the school day. But it got them out of their regular routine, and because it was mandatory, they filled the room each morning.

I spoke on the *one* subject I know anything about: grace. A word that means different things to different people, but to me at least, it is life itself. So I was quite passionate about the task of presenting, defining, and applying this thing called "grace," something that most people in the Muslim world know nothing about. My premise was simple: If I could get them to accept the fact that God might exist and that the Bible is actually reliable, then they should at least consider the words of Jesus. Then, found in His words, and especially in His life, death, and resurrection, they would be confronted with the greatest life-changing reality to ever penetrate the human heart: grace. The premise was simple but the actual implementation of it all would be nothing less than miraculous.

I had not yet done my doctoral work in apologetics (which is basically the study of tough questions of faith), but I knew that's what I would do. I love talking with people who have questions of faith (of course, that would be all of us) and people who are skeptical but sincere about their search. I love hearing people's stories. I've discovered that most Christians would rather have a root canal or be called on to pray spontaneously at some large gathering, but I think it's fun. I feel it's in the midst of spiritual conversations that I find myself on the front lines of where God really is most of the time.

It was an amazing week, and it was nearly over when Samantha and I had the chance to talk privately about her struggles and questions. With much courage and desperation she sought me out to talk, probably because I was getting on a plane a day or two later. It was in that conversation that she said, "Jeff, all this stuff about grace – that God loves me for free, has fully forgiven me, and totally accepts me – is hard to believe." And then she said it: "Jesus is an evil person to me." I asked her how she came to that. Through tears she went on to tell me her story.

The message of God's unconditional love was counter to everything learned in Islam. But it was perhaps harder for Samantha, and she was not Muslim. She was an American who grew up in a Christian home. In fact, her parents were so committed to the calling of God on their lives they had decided to become missionaries in Africa. That's why Samantha was there. That's also why she said what she did. As we talked late into the night, she told me she was a second generation MK. Her grandfather and now her dad were both missionaries.

She was also a second generation child-abuse victim. I know just enough psychology to know there was big time transference going on here. As I talked about her heavenly "Father," all kinds of images came to her mind. They were mostly images of her dad coming off the field, straight from "serving Jesus" and into a rage of violence toward her and her older brother. To say the least, a confusing message was being received by a little girl. And so, on that night under the African moon, she said something out loud that she had only said in her heart, "Jesus is an evil person to me." I understood.

You may be thinking, how could anyone really believe that Jesus is *evil*? That's rather extreme. Is it really? I'm guessing someone reading these words right now has agreed with her, you're just scared to say so.

Many people have a distorted view of the God of the Bible, not because they've actually read it – the Bible – but because they've been hurt like Samantha. And in many cases, it's by those who claim to resemble or at least bear the name of Jesus. Perhaps you have offered the prayer of the little English girl who said, "Lord, please make the bad people good. And make the good people nice." I know I have, many times. Years ago, it was Mahatma Gandhi who said, "I like your Christ, but I do not like your Christians. Your Christians are so unlike your Christ."

I am convinced that if a person truly encounters the *real* Jesus it would be very difficult to reject Him. Of course, all of this runs much deeper than our understanding. It cuts straight to the heart. I've been privileged to see people around the world from all walks of life changed by the power of His love the moment they truly encounter Him. I remember with all the hype of the new millennium, there were many publications looking back over not only the last year or even the last century but the last millennium. *Reader's Digest* ran a cover article that presented Jesus as the most influential figure of the last millennium. I remember thinking, yeah, and the millennium before that too. No doubt Jesus is the central figure of all time. But I wonder how many people really know who He is? Sometimes I wonder if *I* really know who He is. Do you think that your image of Jesus is precisely who He really is? Do you think that you have an accurate understanding of the God of the Bible? Let's go ahead and admit it; if He's really God, we really *don't* know Him as He *really* is. I've come to understand that I don't know anything about God except that which He has chosen to reveal to me. That's why I'm always wary of anyone who claims to have figured it all out.

Jesus said, "If I be lifted up, I will draw all men to me" (John 12:32). Sounds simple, doesn't it? No doubt He was referring to His death on the cross but He was also referring to the proclamation of that event (and who He really is) for millennia to come.

Why aren't all men being drawn to Him? Are Christians not "lifting Him up?" Do we not now have satellite television beaming the message of Christ around the world? Is Christ not "lifted up" every week from pulpits across America and around the world? It pains me to say it, but I don't think so. I think what's being preached today is a far cry from who Jesus really is.

The deluge of pragmatic preaching in our day has left a gaping hole in the theological center of Christianity. In fact, it seems we've forgotten the central core of Christ's message altogether. Think about it. What was the central message of Christ? If you could bring all of the teachings of Jesus to one point what would it be? Love? The Kingdom of God? You might guess by the title of this book, forgiveness? Not exactly. He spoke of these things for sure, but the central focus of His teaching was something else. It seems to me that the central message of Christ was His identity. It was who He *was,* or more correctly, who He *is* that is the entire focus of the New Testament. The thing that set Jesus apart was His identity. It was the focus of all He did. It was the challenge of every debate. It was the shocker of the 1st Century. It was who He claimed to *be* that made Him so unique. And who He claimed to be was why He was nailed to a cross.

Who Jesus was became the central message of those early disciples. It was the one message of the apostolic church. The apostle

Paul said it was the one message he had to preach. Surely it's the one message the Church has today. The one message that can change the world is the message of God's amazing grace wrapped up in His Son and few are really hearing it. Many Christians today seem sidetracked by politics, boycotts, and materialism. We're so busy teaching people how to raise their kids or overcome stress at work that we've missed the one message they need. The one message we have to offer.

This book is for anyone who has struggled to discover the real Jesus. The One you know is there; the One you really want to believe in. The One you've sensed is calling out to you in ways that are too deep for words. Unfortunately, for most of us, it's been a long, hard journey. But be encouraged. It's worth the struggle. My hope is that you will take a step closer to the full reality of God's grace in your life and learn to actually live it. Actually *live forgiven*. That's God's great dream for you. Most Christians I know have never learned to live forgiven. In fact, it seems the more we become indoctrinated, institutionalized, and civilized by today's church, the more we put boundaries around people that will keep them out of the club. The problem is many of us have some huge barriers to overcome. I've concluded there are five main influences in people's lives that keep them from a clear picture of the God of the Bible. Perhaps at least one of them would describe your experience:

1. A lack of exposure to biblical grace
2. Graceless Christians and graceless preaching and teaching
3. Unloving or graceless parents (namely fathers)
4. A misunderstanding of evil and suffering
5. An unwillingness to appropriate the grace of God in relationships

I meet people daily whose lives have been altered by one of the above. Most of us have experienced more than one. I rejoice when people come into our church and say I'm finally home, I feel accepted here, or This feels like a place of grace. Ah, *grace*. There's that word again. I love that word. Philip Yancey calls it the "last best word."[2] Grace means that God loves me just as I am.

Grace means that my worth has been determined by God's love. I am no longer defined by my performance or the approval of others. In his classic book, *The Search for Significance*, Robert McGee puts it this way: I'm totally accepted, fully forgiven, and completely loved by God.[3] I'm defined by something (Someone) beyond myself. I'm defined by grace. Simply put, I'm forgiven.

You're not who you think you are, because God is not who you think He is and He's the One who defines you. So join me as we take a journey, a journey to the heart of God. My hope is as you read these pages you will be taken on a journey of grace. I hope you will discover along with me the greatest truth you'll ever know by getting to know the greatest Person you'll ever know. I hope your journey takes you farther still. I hope you'll learn to actually live in it, or more accurately, live *in Him,* as the apostle Paul loved to say. Perhaps you've been in church all your life but sense there's something missing. Or perhaps you've given up on church because you've been and you left wanting. I've been there too.

Several years ago I had what I call a *grace awakening.* I grew up going to church, but in many ways I somehow missed the greatest truth the church had to offer. In fact, I missed the *only* thing the church really has to offer which is the focus of this book. I found myself in love with Jesus but bored with church. As you take this trip with me, I hope you'll discover what I've discovered. I've never been the same. I've never been more in love with Jesus or, if you can believe this, more excited about His church. I've come to grasp God's amazing love for me, and I've learned that His forgiveness is not only real but it impacts every area of my life. I believe that many people have understood what Christ did on the cross, but very few have truly embraced it as a way of life. So allow this book to be your guide, your friend on your own personal pilgrimage. I hope your experience will lead you to the wide-open spaces known as the fields of God's grace where you can run in the freedom for which you were created. Because whether you know it or not, you've already started this trek.

Section One

You're not who you think you are.

"The only thing worth writing about is the human heart in conflict with itself."
William Faulkner

CHAPTER 1

The Masks We Wear

O ne summer my daughter Emily and I found ourselves in New York City. Truly one of the great cities of the world. As we walked the streets of Manhattan I looked into the eyes of people who had come from all over the world. If they weren't listening to their iPods, they were texting or talking on their cell phones. As we boarded the subway I remembered a sign I had seen years before while in the "tubes" of London that read, "The Museum of Mankind." Surely the subway is a museum of sorts, representing people of all ages, nationalities, and lifestyles. (I think we encountered most of them!) It was a wonderful mosaic of the human race, truly a "museum of mankind."

As I moved among the millions, I thought of the billions more all over the world, in places like Singapore, Seoul, and Sydney. I wondered how many of us really ever discover why we were put on this planet (assuming, of course, we were "put" here)? How many will live eighty or ninety years at best and truly live a life worth living? I know, I know. Jeff, calm down, it's just a fun time with your daughter! Relax, man. Enjoy the sights; ease up a little.

I suppose I should, but I can't. I'm ruined. My life has been wrecked by the grace of God. I so desperately want everyone on the planet to experience this miraculous thing called *grace* that I can't stop thinking about it. In fact, I've given my life to it. It's why I've written this book you're holding. I want you to discover why you were put on this little planet and why your tiny little life really matters. I want you to discover the greatest truth that you will ever know. My hope is that you will be released into the life you've only dreamed of and will embrace it with all you've got.

Why do so many people go through life as if they're just going through the motions? Why do so many of us live from day to day and never experience real joy and purpose in life? And why do so many die having had little impact on the world? Surely you've asked these questions. You may even feel that you've actually discovered some answers that help you sleep at night. Maybe you're truly content with the answers you've received. But don't you sometimes think there's more, that something's missing? If so, it's because some-thing is.

It seems even the worst among us catch glimpses of the eternal: something more, something beautiful, something sacred. I'm sure I'm not the only one who hears the rumblings of something eternal among us. Milton's question echoes across time, "What if earth be but a shadow of heaven?"[4] Why does every culture in the world worship Someone or at least something? Philip Yancey notes in his book, *Rumors*, "Alone of all the beasts, the human animal has the power and freedom to center life in one impulse. We have not, it seems, the power to abstain from worship."[5] What is that within us? Is it simply the result of some evolutionary process that has created within us this God-consciousness, this desire to exalt Someone who is beyond us? Or could it be that God Himself really has "set eter-nity in the hearts of men" (Ecclesiastes 3:11)? Could it be we really do have a kind of "homing device" that calls us onward to seek, to search, to desire? In his classic book, *Mere Christianity*, C.S. Lewis writes, "If I find in myself a desire which no experience in this world can satisfy, the most probable explanation is that I was made for another world."[6] The fact that we have such longings doesn't prove that God is the One prompting us or that eternity awaits, but I believe our longing for Heaven whispers to us in our joy and it seems to scream at us in our despair. Surely you, like me, long for more. Let's see if together we can discover what it is.

The first step on our journey together is for us to realize that we have the wrong impression of ourselves. Who you see in the mirror is not who you are. Put simply, you're not who you think you are. I know you're thinking, Thank you, Jeff, for this blind assessment of my inner self. Stay with me, you're not who you think you are.

My intention here is to take you on a journey that will help you discover who you really are. This is not so much a book about self-discovery as it is about the *greatest* discovery. Socrates was close when he offered his famous two-word summation of the meaning of life: "Know thyself." Knowledge of self is certainly the beginning of an honest self-assessment which should lead to a proper acceptance of oneself. Self-acceptance leads to self-confidence which leads to self-disclosure which should lead to a self-less life of giving to others. Knowing yourself really is a big step toward a healthy, happy life. But Socrates, as smart as he was, missed it. It never really works that way. Though we usually start with self, the answers to life's questions do not begin with me, or anyone else for that matter. They begin with God. Now, I don't claim to be smarter than Socrates, but a lot has happened since he penned those words. A lot and one thing in particular. I'll get to that later.

If it's true that you're not who you think you are, then let's first explore who you think you are. Did that make sense? You think that who you are is what you do. You have measured your worth by your ability to perform in certain areas of your life. At the end of the day, you measure your worth according to your performance. It might be why you're so busy. If you measure your worth by what you do, then the more you *do*, the more you *are*. Time can't increase but your activities do, so you find yourself in over your head. It may also be why your occupation has become your preoccupation. Even when you're not "at work," it's never too far from your thoughts. You can't stand to fail, and so much of your thought life centers on covering the bases so you won't. You're a "human doing" and struggle as a human *being*.

If that doesn't strike a chord, consider your obsession with the opinions of others. Maybe you're an approval addict and you don't know it. I know that sounds extreme, but you probably are more than you realize. You think often about what others are thinking about you. It's why you don't step out of your comfort zone more often. It's why you're slow to reveal your failure or disclose your pain. It doesn't help that many people around you struggle with the same things you do, because they're not talking. You've learned not to talk about it either because that would reveal weakness, and so the cycle continues.

Let's face it, we all wear masks. I love the story I first heard from John Ortberg, of a guy who was desperately looking for work. He couldn't find a job until he went to the zoo where the zookeeper said, "We really don't have any real jobs available but our gorilla just died and you might be able to help us out. If you'll put on this gorilla suit and jump around in the cage like a gorilla, you've got yourself a job." Well, he was smarter than any primate, but he was desperate so he took the job. He was jumping around in the cage, doing his best gorilla impersonation, when he realized the onlookers were quite impressed by what they thought was a real gorilla. He became so excited about his new role that he began swinging from vine to vine. So enthusiastic was he that he flew over the wall and landed in the next cage over, where they keep the lion. As he landed on his back, he had no sooner caught his breath when he felt the hot breath of the lion, who had pounced on top of him. The man could take it no longer. He shouted out in desperation, "Help! Get me out of here!" Suddenly, he heard a voice coming from within the lion. "Be quiet or you're going to get both of us fired!" Evidently there was not an authentic animal in the whole zoo.

Have you ever felt that way? Maybe, like me, you've been shocked by the sudden actions of those you thought you knew. Or perhaps, like me, you've shocked yourself. Sometimes you wonder if there's an authentic person in the whole *zoo*. Have you ever met someone who has courageously discarded the mask? It's a rare and wonderful thing.

Most of us keep our mask on. Many of our masks have smiles on them. They make us look like everything's okay. Some of our masks have frowns or angry scowls. No one would dare get too close to someone who appears disinterested or disconnected. Some of our masks make us look so "together" that people dare not go too deep with us. They don't think we would understand. That's what we want them to think. Some of our masks make us look strong and invincible.

Funny, but sometimes we put on our mask, look in the mirror, and we actually start to believe that's who we really are. But then we fail to perform or we don't receive the approval we thought we would, and then we realize again we're not who we think we are. The truth is, at least at the subconscious level, we knew it all along. We've simply set up so many diversions to real self-discovery that we started to believe we could fix the mess on the inside by cleaning up the outside.

I want to tell you a story. I'll go ahead and tell you, you'll have a hard time believing this one. Years ago I owned a white, two-door Cougar. I bought it used but in good condition. One day I was heading to the office when I got in the car and turned the key. Nothing. Not even a weak turn of the engine. Nothing. Being the expert in automotive repair, I did what every man would do in this situation. I got out of the car, lifted the hood, and poked my head in to take a look. I stared at the complexities of the V-6 engine for about three seconds. I scratched my head and thought about my options. Stacy was gone so I had no other way to get to work. Calling one of my manly friends would be too embarrassing. I couldn't crawl back into bed. Suddenly I had an idea. I pushed the car out of the garage onto the driveway. I went in the garage and pulled out a bucket, some soap, and a hose. For the next hour and a half I was a man on a mission. I rinsed the car, washed it, dried it, and waxed it until it was ready for a Marine boot camp inspection. I cleaned the wheels, shined the tires, and Windexed all the chrome and glass. It was ready for a white glove test. It had never been cleaner. Never had it been so spotless. I got in the car, put the key in the ignition and turned it. Nothing.

Now I was really confused. I got out of the car, stepped back, and looked at it again. I think I said out loud, "Come on! You look great! You look like you're in perfect condition! What's your problem?" Hang with me. I thought for a minute and came up with another plan. If a good cleaning wouldn't do it, perhaps a new image would make her purr like a kitten. "After all," I said, "you look so plain, so boring. You need a new image, a look to call your own!" I decided to draw on my commercial art degree, which to this point in my life had not done me a bit of good. So I ran inside and got my brushes and some paint. I painted a blue racing stripe across the top and the hood. It looked pretty cool but needed something more. I knew just what it was. I painted red, yellow, and orange fire along each side of the white car. It looked awesome. I stepped back and said, "Wow! You look like you're doing a hundred miles an hour just sitting there!" I jumped in the car, turned the ignition…nothing.

By this time I was baffled (and really late for work). If a good outside cleaning and a new image wouldn't do it, what would? I thought for a while and then it hit me. "You need to get a life! You need to do some networking. Look at you. You have the social life of a lawnmower and a couple of trashcans."

Well, suddenly I was a man possessed. I decided to throw a party. I would invite every car within ten miles of our place! I printed up invitations and posted them at every car dealership and garage I could find. If my car wasn't going to get out and make some friends, I'd have to make them for him (her?). Finally the time came for the big party. It was big time! Cars showed up from all over the 'hood. A couple of Hummers recognized each other from the same showroom, a few pickups were making jokes about limited warranties, and a Lexus just stayed over in the corner, not wanting to get too close to anyone, it seemed. All was going well until things got a little out of hand. An old Suburban threw up oil all over the driveway, another drove across my lawn. I'd had enough. After I called it quits and asked everyone to leave, I walked outside only to find empty oil cans all over my front yard. It was disgusting, to say the least.

I got in my car, turned the key and again… nothing! A good cleaning, a new image, even a new social life would not remedy my car's inability to run. Now I know what you're thinking: Jeff, the only thing worse than your sense of humor is your common sense. Who in their right mind would focus on the outside when the problem is on the inside? You might want to read that question again.

We all do it. You've done it. I know I have. Consider the teen-ager desperately seeking acceptance. Looking at the latest teen magazine, she decides she needs a boyfriend. What about the young mom struggling to find herself? "I need a new outfit. I think I'll go shopping. That'll help me feel better," she concludes. "Join a health club," her loving husband suggests. "Maybe you need a new hair-style," a well-meaning friend tells her. How about the middle-aged man, wondering if his life has measured up to his youthful expecta-tions? I'm running out of time, he thinks to himself. Maybe I need a new car, a new job, or… a new wife.

Each one is trying to medicate some particular inner pain or emptiness. And each one focuses on the outside while the problem is on the inside. Why do we do that? It's what we know. It's what we see, or perhaps more importantly, it's what others see. And besides, it's a lot easier to "fix" the outside than it is to fix the inside. Cleaning up the inside takes a lot more work and a lot more time. Change from the inside out is much more challenging than change from the outside in. But, as we usually discover, the latter is really no change at all. Scrubbing the outside is easier than a clearing out of the inside. Rethinking the Source of inner peace and comfort to the human heart takes a lot more time than it does to throw a party. It takes a hard look inside. Something we don't do well. But if you're committed to a life defined by something other than your perfor-mance or the opinions of others, roll up your sleeves. There really is another way to live. But it's going to take everything you've got, *and more*, to make it happen. If you think, *I don't determine my worth by my performance or the approval of others*, read on. You may be surprised at how much you really do.

CHAPTER 2

Getting Off the Roller Coaster

My son, Travis, is simply fascinated with roller coasters. He's at that perfect age where fear and excitement become one. He's old enough to grasp the danger and, at the same time, actually muster up the courage to get on one.[7] And like most kids, he can eat all the food the amusement park has to offer and it doesn't faze him a bit. Have you ever been on a roller coaster? What's so intriguing about a roller coaster is that it goes up and then down with surprising acceleration. Of course, the higher the drop, the more exciting the ride.

That may be fun at some theme park but in real life it's a bummer – for you and everyone around you. Yet most people live their lives on a psychological, and therefore emotional, roller coaster. And though we tend to analyze it all from a psychological or emotional perspective, we've proven that psychoanalysis will not provide the ultimate solution. At its core this emotional roller coaster is a spiritual issue and has only a spiritual solution.

Let me get you started. In order to make an honest self-assessment, I want you to take the "How was your day test." It's real simple and it goes like this: "Did you have a good day today?" You may need to consider yesterday or the past week. I'm serious; work with me. Was it a "good" day or a "bad" day? The answer to that question reveals much about you. I recently posed this question to a large group of young people and asked them to tell me what would constitute a bad day. As you can imagine, especially if you're a young person, their answers went like this: *I didn't do well on a test. My friend was mad at me. I didn't perform well on the court or ball field. My parents were upset with me. My boyfriend broke up with me.*

As I asked what would make up a good day, they responded as you might expect. *I did well on a test. I got a good grade. All my friends seem to like me. My parents are pleased with me. I made the winning touchdown or scored the winning goal.* You see a pattern? Every one of the answers I received had to do with performance or the approval of others.

After years of wrestling with this and guiding others through this journey of significance, I am convinced that most adults on this planet still define themselves in the same way. As a result, billions of us live roller coaster lives that depend upon how well we perform or how much approval we receive on a given day. *I had a productive day. I had the approval of my boss; it was a good day. I lost my job – what a rotten day! I closed the deal I've been working on for months – what a great day! I can tell my spouse is pleased with me; I'm having a good day. Oh, this mirror must make me look ten pounds heavier than I really am! I'm going on that diet… maybe I'll feel better… tomorrow.*

Sound familiar? And so our lives go. Up and down they go. And like the roller coaster, if you stay on that ride for too long, it will make you sick. In fact, counseling centers, psychiatric wards, ministers' offices, and prisons are filled with people sick from their roller coaster existence. Instead of a life of peace and ease they're mostly experiencing a life of dis-ease. In desperate attempts to get off the roller coaster we seek to medicate our pain through endless distractions and diversions. Most people don't even know there's another way to live. Does your life seem like one big cosmic roller coaster ride? Do you sometimes feel you just want to stop the world and get off? What if I told you that it is entirely possible to get off that ride? What if it is actually possible to live a constant and consistent life, no longer made sick by the ups and downs of the fickle opinions of others or your inability to live up to certain standards? It is entirely possible. I know. I've been on that ride. And I got off. I never want to get on it again. Travis has shown the courage to face his fears. We've ridden some pretty cool roller coasters, and there are many more to ride I'm sure. But he's also smart enough to know when to get off. Are you? Read on.

In his book, *The Search for Significance,* author Robert McGee notes that most people can be placed in one or both of two categories. He basically breaks it down to the "performance trap" and the "approval addict."[8] As I referenced earlier, the performance trap leads one to determine his or her self-worth and significance by how well they meet certain standards or by how well he or she performs in certain areas of life. The approval addict determines his or her self-worth by the approval of certain others in his or her life.

Consider the performance trap. If you're caught in the performance trap you feel you must perform well in certain areas because you have come to believe that your significance is determined by how well you perform. If this describes you, it stands to reason that your greatest fear is failure. In fact, that's what drives you – the fear of failure. And therein lies the big problem with the performance-based self-esteem: At some point in life you're going to fail. On the flip side, if you perform well you begin to believe even more strongly that your worth is found through your performance. This leads to one of two things: self-righteousness ("Look how well I'm performing") or an overwhelming need to maintain this "success" through your performance. The first results in a false sense of security, the latter to an even greater need to perform. In fact, most people don't realize that many highly successful people struggle more with the fear of failure than less successful people do. Many well-meaning people have applauded their many successes, further perpetuating their belief and confidence in a performance-based self-esteem. They continue to determine their worth through their performance.

Now consider the approval addict. You're an approval addict if you feel you must have the approval of certain others in your life in order to feel good about yourself. Most often, underneath it all, this need for approval is directly tied to the family of origin and is traced to a parent or parents. My experience in youth ministry and years of counseling men and couples have taught me that most often the need for approval is directly tied to the relationship with the father. This is why the spiritual transference from father to Father is difficult for so many, like with my friend Samantha.

Of course, the big problem with the approval addict is twofold. First, not everyone is going to approve of you; and secondly, those who do approve of you will not approve of you all the time. It stands to reason that your greatest fear is rejection. When the approval addict senses the possibility of rejection he or she will do one of two things: give up and not even try, or do whatever it takes to gain another's approval. This often leads to very unhealthy behavior.

McGee goes on to explain that these approaches lead to the blame game (those who fail are unworthy of love and deserve to be punished) and ultimately to shame (I am what I am. I cannot change. I am hopeless.). Most people live in this downward spiral and are caught in a desperate attempt to define themselves in futile terms.

Much has been written about the performance-based self-esteem and the excessive need for approval with which many people struggle. So let me simply allow you to do some self-discovery. Because the two are so similar and because we're so desperate for significance in life, many of us fall victim to both. There are many factors that increase your propensity toward the performance trap or the need for approval, even both. We all have certain "bents" toward certain attitudes and behaviors, but I think the key is to unlock your past. If your family of origin was driven by significance based on perfor-mance (in school, sports, music, etc.) then you may be a performance freak. If your parents' or others' approval was determined by certain activities or when you conformed to certain behavioral patterns, you may be an approval addict. All of this can happen subconsciously and unintentionally, typically from early childhood.

Consider your own experience. Granted, you have but one limited experience from which to draw, but what do your actions reveal about you? Are there certain areas of your life in which you feel you *must* succeed? Do you find yourself fearing rejection of certain people? Are you driven to perform in certain areas of your life, even to the point of sacrificing important relationships?

What have been the patterns in your life? If your significance is wrapped up in your performance, what do you do when you fail?

Do you have a need to blame others or blame yourself? If you are a high-performance type or perform successfully in certain areas of your life, you may be more susceptible to the roller coaster syndrome than you think. There's a sneaky, undetectable process that lulls you into a fantasy world that will ultimately take you down even further. I've worked with some very successful people and I've observed the more successful a person is in a certain area of life, the more he or she relies on it in order to define their existence.

A young businessman is highly successful, seemingly very healthy. He appears to be quite confident and well-balanced. Suddenly, his company goes south and he's left without a job. His identity has been well established by his success, but now he can no longer claim that identity. The question he's forced to ask is this: *Who am I now?* I've seen parents who define their worth through their children. Once the kids are gone, what then? Again, *Who am I, really?* I think of many successful athletes who have been defined by their sport since grade school. Suddenly they retire at thirty years of age and are forced to ask the question, *Who am I now?* The world of sports is replete with examples of men and women who have struggled to find an answer. Hollywood reveals even more tragic stories.

Ultimately all of this should lead us to some of the deepest questions of life. Why do we live this way? Why does our search for significance most often lead us to performance, the approval of others, blame, and shame? Why do we act out in such weird ways when our ability to perform or gain the approval of others is taken away? And why is it that even "religious" people fall into the same traps? Why do so many Christians adopt this world system and seek to perform for God or try so desperately to gain His approval? Could it be that few of us have ever truly embraced the grace of God and actually learned how to live in it? As shocking as it is, many people go through their entire lives never asking the ultimate questions. Some get desperate enough or sick enough to finally ask the right questions, but they end up doing so in all the wrong places.

I am convinced that the answers to our questions lie not in the field of psychology, sociology, or medicine, but rather in theology. Our ultimate questions and answers are found in the spiritual realm.

You may be thinking, *I don't know much about theology. I'm not a theologian.* Oh, yes, you are. Every person on the planet is a theologian. We all have our own beliefs or non-beliefs about God, and whether you know it or not, it drives everything you do. A. W. Tozer, in his book entitled *The Knowledge of the Holy*, makes this statement: "What comes into our minds when we think of God is the most important thing about us."[9] We'll unpack this one in the next chapter, but I am certain that this is true. Regardless of our view of God, we all have a deep sense within us that He exists. There's no denying it.

Perhaps the reason we often try to squelch this compelling presence is because it's often coupled with another reality that echoes from deep within the human soul. There's something wrong with us. There's a reason I have a bent toward certain behavior that is simply not good for me. There's a reason you and I have thoughts we don't want to have and do things we don't want to do. As hard as we try, we can't overcome this thing that's wrong with us, at least not on our own. There's a longing for something more, a longing to be loved, accepted, approved. And yet, deep within us there's this haunting sense that much of the time we're not too loveable. And as hard as we try to find love on this planet, it seems we're always looking in all the wrong places. We are a part of a greater drama that we can't quite see or fully understand. There's a grand adventure that beckons the human soul. We've been created for so much more and we know it; deep in our spirits we know it.

TIME magazine ran a cover article entitled *The God Gene.*[10] The article asked the question, "Does our DNA compel us to seek a higher power?" As I read the article I immediately thought again of Ecclesiastes 3:11 that says, "God has planted eternity in the hearts of men." Is there something in us that compels us to God? Of course there is, and it runs even deeper than our DNA. The One who created us planted eternity deep within the soul of each of us. Our spirits call out to His Spirit, which is first calling out to us.

Again in his book, *Rumors*, Phillip Yancey points out, "The biblical psalms celebrate the created world as the expression of a Person, a masterpiece of artistic creation worthy of praise. But how can we ascribe beauty to a world assumed to be an accidental by-product of collisions of matter – especially when our sense organs also result from random collisions?"[11] Many of us have lived in this created world and have ascribed creation to something other than the Creator. Yet we see Him in all that is made, we hear Him in every bird, and we feel Him on a sunny day in May. He screams at us every time a baby is born into this world.

In Romans chapter 1, Paul tells us that nature alone screams the existence of God and even reveals His character. He says that the unbeliever is "without excuse," because God has not only revealed Himself in what is seen but He has also "made it evident within them." In the Greek, this literally means inside or within each of us. Once again science is confirming what God told us a long time ago. Each of us has a spiritual "homing device" that draws us to the eternal, to God Himself. We can try to suppress it or deny it but it will not go away. Something (some One) keeps coming back to us whispering, "There is a God; there is a God." This is why I've come to believe that there is no such thing as an atheist in the world. You, like me, may think, hey, I know someone who's an atheist. Well, they may claim to be, but I am certain that the thought of God and the constant wooing of His Spirit are calling out to them "...there is a God....there is a God..." We can either yield to His prompting or we can allow our pride and self-sufficiency to keep us away from Him.

Constantly saying "no" to the reality of God is like the guy who went out and bought himself a new boomerang. He almost killed himself trying to get rid of his old one. It kept coming back to him. As we try to "throw" the thought of God away, He will not let us go. He continues to pursue us. God is in pursuit of every person you know, even the atheist. Now, I do believe there comes a time when God will say to us, *Okay, you don't want to acknowledge My presence in your life? You're on your own. I will let you live as if there is no God.* Perhaps you've been there. Maybe you are now. Perhaps you're a "practical atheist." You believe in God but live as if He doesn't exist. Even now, you lie in bed at night, it gets real quiet, you can find no more diversions, and it comes again, "I am here. I am here." Inevitably a flower blooms, a loved one dies, a sunrise shocks our senses, and we hear it again. It is true; God has done everything He can do to draw us to Himself. He is the Lover who will not give up on His pursuit. But there's a reason why most of us aren't even asking the right questions.

There's a big barrier standing in our way. You see, if knowledge is what you're after, intellectual inquiry will be your guide. If it's a materialistic obsession, then financial acumen will lead you on. And if it's a life of comfort, then the pursuit of pleasure and security will point you to where you want to go. But if it's an encounter with the One who can give you meaning and purpose in life, there's only one way to find Him. And though we've proven a billion times over that none of these other pursuits bring life, we still desperately press on. Perhaps we really believe that somehow we'll be the first of billions to prove everyone else was wrong. There's something wrong with us. Why will we not learn our lesson? What is it that keeps us from the adventure that beckons to us?

CHAPTER 3

True Love is Chosen Love

M ost people underestimate one huge problem that explains why we find ourselves living this roller coaster life. It's a problem the Bible calls "sin." Immediately, some of us don't want to talk about sin as a reality or admit that it is actually at the heart of our problem. It sounds too religious. You think I'm now going to start preaching, because sin has been used by many as a whip in order to present some superior religious position. Interestingly, our resistance and aversion to take sin seriously is actually evidence of it. No one likes to talk about it. We struggle to admit our failures and we struggle to confess our sins. Instead, we try to hide them, which again underscores the fact that we seek significance through our performance and the approval of others. It is true that we are only as sick as our secrets. If you can't talk about it, it's already out of control. Shouldn't that serve as a sign to us? Something's wrong.

The reality of sin is ever before us, and any intellectually honest person, spiritual or otherwise, would have to agree that the Bible offers the best solution for our problem. And, as we'll discover on this journey together, the *only* solution. Some have tried to define it all in sociological, psychological, or educational terms. But at the end of the day, after all the debates over educational or sociological solutions are over, we go home and watch the news and we're reminded again that we live in a very sinful world. Something more than a genetic mishap or environmental collapse is taking place. If education or economic acumen was the solution, our nation would surely be one of the most morally upright countries in the world. Clearly we are not, which does not bode well for our "Christian nation." As someone has noted, a thief with an education is just an educated thief. A pedophile with a doctorate is, well, "Dr. Pedophile."

Let's be honest, we really don't have to watch the evening news. We can simply look in the mirror and reflect on our own personal pilgrimage. Each of us is on a downward, southbound, gravitational pull toward sin. Whatever you want to call it, you know you can't shake it on your own. Humans have proven it throughout history and you've proven it experientially in your life as well. I know I have. Any effort to deal with it apart from God simply leads to a denial of reality or a life wrought with the constant pursuit of the next unsuccessful diversion.

The problem with our culture is that we have eliminated the answer before asking the question. It is as if the number four doesn't exist. What then is two plus two? It might be three, or perhaps five. But it can't be four; there is no such thing. If you eliminate the answer before you ask the question, it always leads to absurdity. After all of our "enlightened" debates, if we dare to come back to the Bible, everything suddenly makes sense. In fact, as I've studied world religions I've found that none of them give an answer to the problem, much less the solution to sin. And though I don't define Christianity as another "religion" (more on that later), it is only in Christianity that we find a comprehensive solution to this problem of sin.

It seems the popular approach to religion these days is to see all roads as leading to the same God. Somewhere along the way we even tossed out Aristotle's "law of non-contradiction" and have come to believe that two opposing ideas that say two different things altogether can somehow both be right. I've talked to many people who have come to believe that the key to understanding life is to draw from all religions (or maybe none) and come up with a hodge-podge of "truth" that they think is best. Most people who approach life this way have not thought this through to its logical conclusion. This kind of thinking ultimately leads to absurdity. The logic goes something like this: Surely no *one* religion can hold all truth (that would be way too exclusive or absolute), so the truth must be found by taking from the very best of all religions.

It all sounds enlightened and inclusive until you ask the question, how do you determine what is *good* or *best* from each religion? What standard do you use by which to judge what is good or best? Anyone who stops to think about the answer to that question will ultimately see where it leads. You become your own god, deciding what is right and what is wrong.

Could there be any more self-righteous or self-centered approach to life? You form your own religion, philosophy, or worldview with "guess who" at the center of it. Ironically, those who seek to be inclusive and keep truth relative suddenly realize they're doing what they find so narrow-minded in others; namely, claiming they have the right or authority to define what is "truth." Wouldn't it stand to reason that one religion, not three or four or all of them, would have a more connected and comprehensive body of truth that would make a lot more sense taken altogether?

Let me show you how simple the truth really is. The Bible says simply, "All have sinned and fallen short of the glory of God" (Romans 3:23). Again, no self-aware person would have much trouble with that bit of truth. Notice that sin is actually falling short of a particular standard. Here it's called the "glory of God." That is to say the "righteousness," or simpler still, the "perfect-ness" of God. This is worth noting: sin is not simply failure to live up to God's perfect standard, but it is, in fact, our *inability* to live up to God's perfect standard. I'm thinking why has God set it up this way? Why is this thing called *sin* such a huge problem? Some may ask why do I *need* to be forgiven? Let's explore the truth that most people have missed.

The Bible says, "God is love." And yet, for many, this truth is hard to believe. It seems difficult to reconcile a loving God and the reality of sin. And yet many who don't believe in sin or the idea that we really need forgiveness, don't realize that the reality of sin actually leads us to the love of God. Hang with me. Every atheist, agnostic, or unbelieving person has a story to tell. Every atheist or person antagonistic toward God will share the story of a wound from their past. For many it's a deep wound.

I remember speaking to a group of students at a summer camp. After I spoke, a young man about 16 years old wanted to talk. He was one of those kids that had it written all over him; he was angry. He said that even the thought of God makes him angry, and he could not believe in the loving God that I was talking about. He then rattled off question after question about why a loving God could allow this or that to happen. I realized that this could go on all night and it probably would. After hours of addressing his questions he wouldn't be any closer to trusting this God he was so mad about. Through my years of student ministry I've learned to cut to the chase. So I asked him to tell me about his relationship with his dad. Before I knew it this strong, aggressive young man was weeping. He was no longer on the offensive. He was suddenly weak and tired. He told me that his dad thinks he works out all the time because he plays football. But through tears he told me he actually works out so his father wouldn't beat him anymore. For years he had looked forward to the day when he would be stronger and bigger than his father so the beatings would stop and he would finally be set free from the hell of his childhood. We talked into the night and then sought to begin a process of healing with those who knew and loved him. I knew his freedom would not come easily.

I tell this story because all of us have one. You may think, well, that's kind of extreme. For some it is, but who has not asked, if God is so loving, why is there so much evil in the world? This question is asked in different forms, born out of our own experience. Why do children experience abuse? Why do parents not stay together? Why are innocent people murdered? Why did cancer take my loved one?

Sometimes questions can only be answered with questions. I was talking to a young husband who was struggling to believe in a loving God in the face of evil and suffering. I said, "Give me a better world." Of course, the quick answer is, "Okay, I've got your better world. How about a world where children don't die, people aren't killed, and families stay together?" My response was a bit shocking: "Now you're asking for a world where there is no love." "How's that?" "Well, it's simple," I said, "because true love is chosen love." In a world where love is possible there must be choice. This is perhaps the greatest gift of God to us. God in His infinite wisdom has given us the dignity to choose, knowing that many would choose against Him. Why? The answer is obvious. More than anything else, God wants you and me to choose to love Him. So He has given us a choice. Our God is no puppeteer but a Lover of His creation. You and I are free to love God or not to love God. A world without choice is a world without love. Sin is simply the result of our choosing not to love God.

Let me ask you a question that will help bring even more clarity to this thing called sin. Do you believe that God can do anything? Think about it. Of course, the quick answer is yes. I used to believe that until I came to this problem of evil and suffering in the world. Here's the question: Can God create a world in which we are free to love and where sin does not exist? I think not. You see, because true love is chosen love, such a place could not exist except in heaven. Love can be present only where there is a choice to love, and with that choice there must be the possibility for something else. That "something else" is what the Bible calls sin. In fact, Karl Barth, the great German theologian, defined sin as simply choosing other than good, other than God. The question at hand is like asking, *Can God create two mountains with no valley between them?* The real answer is it can't be done. It's not that God can't do it, it's simply illogical; it can't exist. It may be surprising for you to hear me say that I do not believe that God can do *anything*. He can, however, do anything that *can* be done. So it is with a world in which we are free to love where sin does not exist. It can't happen. Again, give me a better world. There is none or God would have created it.

Here's the point: You and I live in the perfect environment in which to choose to love God. This great gift of choice began when God made His own choice about you. Long before your choice to love or reject God, God chose to love you. "This is love. Not that we love God, but that He first loved us and sent His Son as an atoning sacrifice for our sins." (1 John 4:10) You have been given the opportunity to respond to the God who has created you. He has demonstrated His love for you so that you might respond to His love and live in it. We can determine to define ourselves through our performance or the approval of others, or we can choose to live in His love and be defined by it. There really *is* another way to live.

If all of this talk of God and sin and choice has got your head spinning, let me challenge you to think about a new way to live. In fact, I hope you'll keep on reading, because my purpose here is to show you how to live in a new way. I want you to live forgiven. Instead of living the rest of your days bouncing up and down on thoughts and emotions based on outward happenings, you can actually live a life centered on an inward happening. Again, it's a life based on something that's *already* happened. You and I were created to live a life in which grace has happened and continues to happen until the day we die. This is the life you were born to live, and it can be yours if you choose it. It's a life of consistency, because your worth is based on a never-changing source of grace. You begin to define your worth by that which has already happened *in* you not that which happens *to* you. Your failures are swallowed up in forgiveness and your successes are met with humility. Shame is covered by the love of God and pride is swallowed up by a deep sense of gratitude for that love. The opinions of others take a backseat to the One whose opinion matters, and you become quick to forgive, releasing yourself to a joy-filled life.

CHAPTER 4

Jump

I think the biggest barrier you will face as you consider living forgiven is fear. Living in the grace of God is scary for most because we've never been there before. It's a complete shift in our thinking, a new paradigm. Perhaps the scariest part of this new way of living is that it requires a complete dying to self. This is where the fear comes in. We want to be in control. Often in our world, this need for control appears to be a sign of power, but in reality it's a sign of weakness. Put in biblical terms, it's a lack of faith. And guess what the opposite of faith is? It's not disbelief, it's fear; though the two are intricately connected. As I've noted, the answers to life's greatest and most important questions are found in the theological realm. This is where most people struggle because any time you enter into the realm of the theological you are entering into the realm of faith.

Again, you may respond with, *Well, I'm not a very religious person.* It may surprise you, but I'm not either. I *am*, however, a man of faith. Religion is trusting in our own efforts to get us to God, which will never happen because of sin. Faith, on the other hand, is trusting in what God has already done for us. This is what separates Christianity from every other religion in the world. Religion is man's effort to get to God. Christianity is God's effort to get to us. The roller coaster ride is over. You can get off. In fact, much of this book is about how to appropriate the greatest theological truths you'll ever know, which are presented in the next chapter. But let me warn you again, your biggest hurdle will be fear. Because, for many, I'm talking about a new way to live.

Do you know what the most common command in all of Scripture is? To love others? To forgive? To obey God? None of these. Knowing the human condition and our propensity toward fear, God's number one command is "Fear not," and "Don't be afraid." You find it no less than 366 times in the Bible. Someone has noted that's one per day for the year and one extra for leap year. God wants us to be reminded daily, *Don't be afraid, you can trust Me.* The human heart has a bent towards fear. I've seen a major shift in my lifetime – the post 9/11 world is a world of fear.

As I write this, I just walked through customs at LAX airport. Connecting from an international flight to a domestic flight took two hours. Perhaps you've done the drill. I took off my shoes, watch, belt, and emptied my pockets, while all of my bags were X-rayed. All because we fear someone is evil enough to want to do harm to those of us on the plane.

Overcoming our fears has become a national pastime, or at least the subject of our favorite movies and TV shows. We all have certain phobias. Some are common. Perhaps you've heard of arachnophobia, the fear of spiders; or claustrophobia, the fear of confined spaces; or aerophobia, the fear of flying. Others are less common, like dentophobia, the fear of dentists; glossophobia, the fear of speaking in public (which is ahead of the fear of death, by the way); paraskavedekatriaphobia, the fear of Friday the thirteenth; pentheraphobial fear of your mother-in-law (I'm not kidding); and bigdaddywithabatphobia, the fear of your father-in-law (okay, I made that one up). Acrophobia? The fear of heights. Ecclesiophobia? The fear of church. The list goes on and on. As we walk through this journey together you'll have to face your fears. Dorothy Thompson, the first American journalist to be expelled from Nazi Germany, said, "Fear grows in darkness; if you think there's a bogeyman around, turn on the light." I want to help you turn on the light, but you'll be the one to turn the switch. One of your greatest fears may be the fear of discovering that you've had the wrong idea about yourself all along. And fear can keep you from the greatest life you'll ever know. So

I'm asking you to dive in. In order to live forgiven, you'll need to jump.

Several years ago, in a sudden lapse of judgment, I went on a campout with a group of senior guys who were about to graduate from high school. I was supposed to provide the adult presence. We camped out (if you call sleeping on the ground without tents "camping") at Possum Kingdom Lake, just west of the Dallas/Fort Worth metroplex. The next morning I should have been a little concerned when one of the guys announced our arrival at "Hell's Gate." Imagine looking over a majestic lake from atop a cliff that drops straight down to the water – 90 feet below. It was breathtaking, gorgeous, a spectacular view. Now imagine, and remember you're with senior boys, that this rare moment of awestruck inspiration is interrupted when someone issues the challenge: "Let's jump."

"Jump?" I asked. I stood as close as possible to the cliff and looked down. Jump! Then one of the guys added, "What, are you scared?" The next thing I knew about four of us were standing on the edge daring the other to go first. Finally we devised a plan. We would all jump together, at the same time. "On three," I said. And together we shouted, "One, two, three!" And *no one* jumped! We all looked at each other, using appropriate names to decry each man's fear.

On about the third time of that same routine, we did it. We jumped. It was terrifying, exhilarating, even liberating. In fact, after the first jump, guess what I did? You got it. I climbed up the cliff eager to do it again... and again...and again. Why? It was a rush, for one. But it was also for further confirmation. I had conquered fear. And once you conquer fear and experience what you might have otherwise missed, you respond with even greater acts of faith. Not so much in defiance but more out of a sense of gratitude. By the third time I was running off the cliff.

Don't you think it's time for you to jump? Perhaps you've seen the grandeur of God. You've sat atop the cliff, moved by the beauty below. Perhaps you've actually seen others jump. You may know a jumper. Even now, you may know someone who seems to live this grace-filled life you've been thinking about. You've thought, *That's great for them but that's just not me.* A few times you've even thought about jumping. Maybe you're holding this book because you know that in the midst of this one and only life, there's got to be more. Perhaps God has led you to a point where you find yourself standing at the edge. You're ready to jump but you don't know how. Your knees are shaking because you actually think you just might be ready.

On a wall in my house next to my kids' rooms is a close-up picture of a giant lion's face. Below the picture it says, "Courage is not the absence of fear but the determination to do what is right in the face of it." That's how I want my kids to live. That's how I want to live. I think you do, too. Before you jump, let me remind you: you're not who you think you are, and God is not who you think He is, either.

Questions to ponder:

1. As you think about how you determine your value and worth, what do you have a tendency to rely on the most- your performance or the approval of others? In what ways have you seen this in your life?

2. Have there been times in your life when you have focused on the "outside" while the problem was really on the "inside?" What did you do? What did you learn?

3. Has your life ever felt like a roller coaster? Have you ever experienced times when you felt like you were *not* on it? When was that and why do you think that was?

4. Name some examples in our culture in which people have denied or even underestimated the reality of sin.

5. Explain the statement, "True love is chosen love" in your own words.

Section Two
God is not who you think He is.

"What comes into our minds when we think of God is the most important thing about us."
A. W. Tozer

CHAPTER 5

The God You've Been Looking For

The reason you're not who you think you are is because God is not who you think He is. Ultimately all of life begins and ends with God and everything is defined by Him. In fact, apart from Him life makes no sense and has no purpose. It follows that if we believe the wrong things about God we'll have misunderstandings about who we are and what we are to think and do in this life. Let's just go ahead and be humble and human enough to admit it: God is not who I think He is. I say this not because I know your spiritual pilgrimage. I say this because I am certain that God is holier than you could ever comprehend. He's more loving than you could ever know. He's more powerful than you could imagine and His grace reaches farther than any of us could ever grasp. He's bigger than our minds can fathom. Reflect again on Tozer's statement: "What comes into our minds when we think of God is the most important thing about us." God is not like us.

Every summer for the past nine years I've been privileged to speak at a Christian family ranch called Wind River Ranch. It's become a part of the fabric of our family's history and a source of our very best memories together. This past summer I was reminded that every time I find myself in the Rockies I'm amazed at the beauty and sheer size of the mountains. I realize again how small I am and I get "right-sized" real quick.

One night we went to the upper meadow where I saw more stars than I'd ever seen in my life. I was awestruck. I remembered summer nights as a kid watching shooting stars while lying on a pier at Lake Norman, just outside of Charlotte, North Carolina. We would count them late into the night. But what I saw in Colorado was a completely different version of the same show. It was big screen, high definition by comparison. My girls were lying in the meadow with some friends and saw a shooting star that was so ablaze with light and color they first thought it to be fireworks. There was a collective scream of excitement and appreciation (worship) by everyone who saw it.

Then the next night, all alone, I stared up at the sky, praying. Immediately struck by how small I am, it was one of those rare moments when I was praying without words. I was, in fact, silenced by the presence of the Almighty. It was an amazing time of awe and wonder. I can only describe it as communion with God, rare and often difficult to find, but impossible to deny.

I've never been an astronomy geek, but that night I began a curious exploration of what I was seeing (and what I wasn't seeing) as I gazed into the heavens. It became very clear to me that I am one tiny little human on a tiny piece of real estate called the Rocky Mountains on a tiny little planet called Earth in a tiny galaxy known as the Milky Way. In a strange way I felt very insignificant and very special at the same time.

What I've since learned is that I was looking at our galaxy of stars that is so huge that even at the speed of light it would take up to 200,000 years to travel across it. You may remember that one light-year is the distance that light can travel (in a vacuum) in one year which equals 5.88 trillion miles – that's 186,282.397 miles per second!

Try to wrap your mind around this. You realize that every star, every little speck out there, is a sun. And most stars are larger than our sun. Our sun is 93 million miles away (about 8 light minutes), but it's so bright and its heat so strong, it only takes 8 minutes for you to feel it hit your face – from 93 million miles away. It would take 333,000 Earths to make up the size of our sun. The Earth is almost 8,000 miles in diameter. The sun is 862,000 miles in diameter. 109

Earths could be lined up horizontally across the middle of the Sun. Now, that's just *one* star; and a relatively small one at that!

Hang with me as we continue our astronomy class. A galaxy is like an island in space made up of gas, dust, and billions of stars. Our own galaxy, the Milky Way, includes about a trillion (a thousand billion) stars in a disk shape. A few years ago the Hubble Space Telescope took an image called the "Hubble Deep Field." The image was one spot of sky near the Big Dipper about the width of a dime 75 feet away. Scientists looked at that small segment of space – in that little area – and counted over 1,500 galaxies! Take that number times the volume of space in every direction, and you would calculate that there are millions of billions of galaxies with billions, even trillions, of stars in each galaxy! Now we're into numbers that we can't even grasp. But let's try; or at least blow our minds trying.

A trillion is a million millions. It can be described this way: One million dollars would equal a stack of $100 bills that would be over six feet high. If you made a stack of $100 bills that would equal a one trillion dollar pile, it would be 40 times higher than Mount Everest. Mount Everest peaks at over 29,000 feet. Your stack would be somewhere around 220 miles high. Let me say that again – there are billions of galaxies with trillions of stars in each.

While lying on my back looking up at the Colorado sky I couldn't see the Orion constellation or other galaxies like the famous Andromeda Galaxy. It's over 2.4 million light-years away from us. (Again, 186,000 miles per second – almost 6 trillion miles in a year = a light-year.) You clip along for 2.4 million of those and you get to the Andromeda Galaxy. It's 220,000 light-years across.

There is a lot more out there that I didn't see. I couldn't see the Eagle Nebula (gas and dust in space) or the Ring Nebula – 1,500 light-years from one side to the other. That's 30 times the distance between the Earth and the sun. I realized that, perhaps for the first time in my life, I was beginning to understand (or experience) verses like Psalm 19:1: "The heavens declare the glory of God; the skies proclaim the work of His hands." Our God is not like us. No wonder the psalmist cried out, "O Lord, our Lord, how majestic is Your name in all the Earth! You have set Your glory above the heavens" (Psalm 8:1).

Scientists now concede that the only limit to the universe is our ability to observe it. They've admitted that the numbers they use are simply another way of saying, even in scientific terms, the universe is infinite. My son, Travis, and I recently viewed an IMAX presentation on black holes (at the Air and Space Smithsonian museum – you've got to think guys might know something). After a half an hour of amazing computer-generated images and a lot of scientific/ philosophical language, I walked out thinking, "They have no idea what a black hole is." I ask you again, what might God's creation tell us about Him? The God you're looking for is bigger than you think.

CHAPTER 6

Finding Him

Okay, so God is big. But can we really find Him, even know Him? Remember my friend Samantha in the introduction? How can someone describe Jesus as "evil"? Most people would consider her conclusions unfounded and, in fact, far from the truth. Clearly she had a story behind her ideas about God. You have a story too. I want the next few pages to serve as an exercise similar to one I walked through in graduate school when a systematic theology professor challenged us toward a process he called "theological reconstruction." The idea is that each of us has presuppositions and preconceived ideas of who God is and what He is like. And for most of us, our ideas are wrong. Perhaps you need to reconstruct your own theology.

In the following pages I want to challenge you to think about who God really is and what He is like by entering into a kind of "theological reconstruction." For some it may be more of a theological "deconstruction." Sometimes we need to tear down before we can build again. Perhaps you're thinking seriously and critically about your own theology for the first time. Often, for those who have grown up in church, it can be a much more difficult task than those who didn't.

A question I've heard often is how do I know which god is the right God? Which God are we looking for? There's only one God. The God you're looking for is the same God who has revealed

Himself throughout history. You may have asked, *What if the Bible is really not the "Word of God"*? What if the story of Christ is just a blown-up tale about a man who lived but never really did any of those things in the Bible? What if the suffering in your life has no meaning at all? What if there were no God behind all the order and design, the beauty and majesty of the universe?

What if there's no need for forgiveness because there's no *right* or *wrong*, no moral absolutes? What if it really is just everyone's opinion against everyone else's opinion? What if there is no "love"? Without a loving, Divine Creator, love is reduced to an evolved chemical reaction or animal instinct. Without a Divine Creator, we have no soul. And without a soul there is no eternity so life is over when you die and there is no greater purpose or meaning to this life.

But what if there is a God who created you and who has a divine purpose in everything? What if He really has revealed Himself to you? What if the Bible really is His Word, and what if He has actually come to us in the Person of Jesus Christ? What if it's true? What if He really is so big and so "other" than we are, the only way we could come to Him is by faith? What if the Bible is completely true and Jesus really died on the cross as the One and Only perfect Lamb of God who has taken away the sins of the world? And what if that gift of forgiveness is not forced on you but rather one you can choose for yourself to receive? What if faith really is the gateway to forgiveness, purpose, and hope? What if it's all bigger than you can even grasp? What if you must first believe before you can really understand? What if there is a God who has a Master plan that we cannot always see? What if there's coming a day when all that we can't quite grasp will make sense? What if God really is in control of everything? The Bible says that this is the reality of our world. Do you believe this? I'm convinced of it. In the end, it's the only world view that makes sense at all.

As we explored in Section One, all of us have certain assumptions about who God is and what He's like. As you continue in the process of reconstructing your theology, consider how God has revealed Himself to us. Let's see if your conceptions of God match up with how He has actually revealed Himself. If they don't, it may be worth asking, *Who's wrong?* You see, we start not with ourselves, but with God. The only thing we know about Him is what He has chosen to reveal to us. We know nothing else. So, how has He chosen to reveal Himself to us? I'd suggest there are five key ways God has revealed Himself to us so that we might find Him.

General Revelation

God may be indescribable, but He is not unknowable. As we've already considered, God has revealed Himself to us through creation. Theologians call this "general revelation." He is seen "in general" throughout all of creation. Through it all we catch a glimpse of who He is. Creation reveals who He is – His character, His beauty, His "bigness", and I think how "small" He can be as well. God reveals Himself in general terms through His creation so that humans will simply humble themselves before Him and then partner with Him to accomplish His purposes. God doesn't reveal Himself for kicks. He reveals Himself on purpose, or even *for* His purpose. Simply put, God's job is to do the revealing, ours is to do the responding. We respond to His revelation by humbling ourselves before Him and surrendering our lives to Him.

So the logical question is this: What does creation say about who God is? And regardless of where you are in your faith journey, doesn't it seem logical that God created all that is? Remember, it is scientifically impossible to get something out of nothing. In regard to the Aristotlean logic of "cause and effect," there must be a cause for every effect. Ultimately you are led to an "Uncaused Cause." What does creation reveal to us about who God is? What can we know about Him?

Throughout all He has made God shows us how wonderfully creative He is and how thoroughly involved He is with His creation. He cares for His creation and in ways and in places that we have never seen or thought about. When the Discovery Channel presented its series, *Planet Earth*, it quickly became a favorite in our family. Taking years to make, a group of British scientists and photographers put together, what was for me at least, one worship sequence after another. As they show us places and practices in creation never before seen, we're reminded that much of God's creation and caring seems, at times, gratuitous, unnecessary, even extravagant.

For instance, why didn't He stop at 100 billion stars? Why did He create billions of galaxies with trillions of stars in each one? Why didn't He stop at 2,000 mammals? (There are 4,260 different types of mammals.) There are 6,787 species of reptiles, nearly 10,000 different types of birds and 28,000 species of fish. And, of course, invertebrates outnumber all the vertebrates put together. There are 80,000 species of mollusks and a million different kinds of insects. Why didn't He stop at 1,000 types of insects? I read recently that there are 300,000 species of beetles and weevils alone! What's up with that? Again, what does this say about God? As a piece of art expresses the heart of the artist, God's artwork, His creation, is an expression of who He is.

Why the extravagance, the lavish and seemingly excessive creativity? Some scientists have now added to their reasons for the existence of such a vast universe this interesting thought: The universe exists so that we might explore it and in so doing find the One who is the Creator of it all. Again, He's not just "out there." He wants to be found by us.

It's as if He is trying to say to us throughout His creation that He is the One in control of all of life – not us. It's as if He wants us to know who's in control, as if to say, "You're going to need a God like me. You're going to need a God who creates and cares for His creation in ways that you don't even see. You're going to need a God who gives and blesses and sustains and loves for seemingly no reason whatsoever." That's the kind of God He is. He loves because that's who He is, and we see His heart in creation.

The Revelation of His Word

I've talked to people about all kinds of varied beliefs about God. When I ask, how did you come to believe that, I get a variety of answers. "A friend of mine once told me..." or "I read somewhere..." or more commonly, "I was watching this show on TV and ..." It seems there are as many opinions as there are people. The problem with so many is that even if we've been thoughtful enough to ask the right questions, we've been asking in all the wrong places.

We need a reliable source, one that makes sense, that's comprehensive in its scope and practical in its approach. Thanks be to God, that's exactly what the Bible is. It is His source of truth for us in all of life. We don't have to wonder what God is like because He's told us.

The God of creation is the God of the Bible who has come to make Himself known to us. So what does God's Word say about who He is? A lot. This representative passage from Psalm 8 says, "O Lord, our Lord, how majestic is your name in all the earth! You have set your glory above the heavens. From the lips of children and infants You have ordained praise...when I consider Your heavens, the work of Your fingers, the moon and the stars, which You have set in place, what is man that You are mindful of him?..." Above all creation, God has chosen us (you) to display His "glory." His glory is the expression of His character, His essence. Ponder this: *You* are at the pinnacle of His creation. You are an image-bearer of God, filled with the potential for the greatest acts of love, virtue, and self-sacrifice. We have within us the potential for incredibly noble lives filled with a declaration of His glory. In fact, that's why you were created – to display His glory. His character, the expression of His glory, is to come through your life.

The Ultimate Revelation of Jesus

He's revealed Himself in creation and in His Word, but He's revealed Himself with the greatest clarity through His Son, Jesus. When asked how do I know God exists I'll often say because He came here and told us so. Jesus was God in the flesh. The entire purpose of the Bible is to point us to Jesus and show us how to worship Him with our lives. God's highest expression of glory was revealed in and through Jesus Christ. So what does Jesus Christ say about who God is? Everything left unsaid. Hebrews 1:3 puts it this way, "The Son is the radiance of God's glory and the exact representation of His being, sustaining all things by His powerful Word. After He had provided purification for sins, He sat down at the right hand of the Majesty in heaven." This is why I'd like to suggest that Jesus alone is worthy of your life. He calls us to die to ourselves and live for Him. We were created for God, not for ourselves. You and I were created to display His glory.

The Revelation of His Present and Tangible Body

God reveals Himself in another way that will come as a surprise to some. God reveals Himself through His Church. I'm not talking about a building where some local church gathers near your house. I'm talking about the collective members of the family of God. God reveals Himself through His people. Just as Jesus was the Incarnation of God (literally, God "in the flesh"), the Bible says that His followers are the Incarnate presence of Himself (His "Body") in the world today. From the time Jesus left the earth physically, His people have been His presence on our planet. He reveals Himself to us through His Spirit which is alive in every person who has been forgiven by Him and has chosen to live in Him. The apostle Paul wrote, "Now you are the body of Christ, and each one of you is a part of it." (1 Corinthians 12:27) This happens as His followers "die" to themselves and live for Him. Again, Paul put it this way, "I have been crucified with Christ and I no longer live, but Christ lives in me. The life I live in the body, I live by faith in the Son of God, who loved me and gave Himself for me." (Galatians 2:20)

His Up Close and Personal Revelation

So the logical question, if you consider yourself a lover of God, is this: What does *my* life say about who God is? You see, you have a choice every day of your life. You can choose to live out of the *smallness* of who you are or out the *bigness* of who God is. God is bigger than you think, and every day you have the choice to either live out of the greatness of God or you can go on living out of the smallness of who you are. We can choose to live earthbound lives, tethered to our sinful bent and follow after our puny little dreams, or we can decide that we will allow the Creator of it all to breathe into our puny little lives the very breath of God that gives us life. We can choose to live as children of the King with access to all the resources of heaven.

How will you choose to live? Whatever challenge you are facing in your life you can choose to be faithful to God or you can trust in your own puny efforts. You can have a *me-sized* approach to life and say, *I can't do that*, or you can have a God-focused faith that brings forth a God-sized vision and dream for your life. God is longing for someone to believe Him for who He really is – this big, limitless, untamable, unshakable, unfathomable God. He is just waiting to reveal His glory through your life. And it is your "yes" to Him that opens the door to the unlimited potential of His power in your life. I'm talking about partnering with Him doing this life together. He's not who you think He is. He's bigger than you think, but He's also closer than you think.

CHAPTER 7

Missing the Point

ᏁᎩ

Now that we've seen how this knowable God has revealed Himself to us, let's consider how we respond to Him. As we delve into what *you* believe about God, we must consider what "belief" or "faith" in God really is. I don't know where or how you came to believe what you believe about God, but all of us have misconceptions about who God is. I know this is true, because biblically speaking, belief is not just hoping that something is true or even agreeing intellectually that something is true.

Why is faith so hard for us? In part, because most of us have a misunderstanding of what faith really is. Even our dictionary betrays our understanding as it lists faith as a noun. Biblical faith – the kind with which we must come to God – is really a verb. It's not simply something you possess but something you do. And before you think you're not a person of faith consider that the next time you turn the key in your car or walk into a room and flip the light switch. Faith is acting on something even though you don't completely understand it. You do it all the time. Spiritually speaking, faith is hard because it always requires that we let go of our own control of things.

I've received help from many people as I've struggled with faith throughout my Christian experience. One such person lived about 800 years ago. Anselm of Canterbury was a leading theologian of the 11th Century. His understanding of faith has challenged mine and brought clarity to my mind and peace to my heart. To grasp his teaching, consider two statements. Which is truer? *I believe, therefore, I understand,* or *I understand, therefore, I believe.* If you consider yourself one who believes, how did you come to believe? Did you first understand then believe, or did you believe and then understanding followed? And wasn't that belief actually tied to something you *did*?

"My teaching is not my own," Jesus said in John 7:16-17. "It comes from Him who sent me. If anyone chooses to do God's will, he will find out whether my teaching comes from God or whether I speak on my own." Notice that biblical belief has a particular sequence: Choose to do God's will and the assurance and the confidence, everything we tend to base belief on, will follow. Anselm's point was this: Faith will always precede reason in our relationship with God. Christianity *is* rational, but faith will always come before reason. I act on what I believe, *then* understanding comes. The Bible teaches us that God always insists that we trust and obey Him, *then* knowledge will follow. Perhaps this is, in part, why you've struggled with faith. You have thought it's a thing you'll *grasp* or *understand* some day. You're hoping and waiting but greater faith has not come. And it will not; not until you act on the truth that God has already revealed to you (more on what truth I'm talking about in a moment).

In the end, it's not so much what you believe about God that interests me (or Him) but what you actually *do* with that belief. What you *do* reveals more about what you believe than what you *say* you believe. It is true that most Christians need to move more toward *faith* than *facts* and more toward *actions* than *beliefs*. Some may argue if people don't have proper beliefs they won't know how to act. I'm certain this is true but what I see most often are people who seem to have all the right beliefs with little or no impact on the way they actually live. This is precisely what Jesus spoke against the most. In fact, it drove Him nuts. It's why the book of James essentially says, "You don't have to tell me what you believe. I'll know what you believe by what you do." Don't be fooled. Faith without action is not faith at all.

Maybe your spiritual life is a lot like the woman who came to a pastor and told him she didn't love her husband anymore. In fact, she was going to get a divorce as soon as possible. Not only did she want out of the relationship, she wanted to make her husband pay for all the pain and frustration he had caused her. The wise pastor told her, "For the next three weeks I want you to do everything you know your husband loves for you to do. Please him in every way. Make his favorite meals; go to his favorite places. Say all the things you know he wants you to say." The woman responded, "You don't understand. I said I want to get rid of him. I want out of this relationship!" The pastor said, "I know. Just do what I've said and after three weeks just pull the rug out from under him. You give him all that he wants and then just strip it all away from him. That'll show him!" After three weeks the woman came back to the pastor, this time with her husband. Their big smiles expressed their gratitude as they thanked the pastor for saving their marriage. They had never been more in love. The pastor knew it would happen. He believed a biblical principle that works in all of life: It's easier to act your way into a new way of feeling than to feel your way into a new way of acting. In fact, I've learned that sometimes faith really is like acting *as if* I believe, even when I'm not sure I do. Often psychologists practice this sequence in therapy. This approach follows the belief that we change behavior by acting *as if* a particular desired state is true. We act our way toward a new way of thinking.

Now, you may hear this and think, Okay, so you're telling me to *pretend* it's all true and just act accordingly. No, faith is not pretending or crossing our fingers in hopes that something is true. Faith is not wishful thinking. Here's why: Faith is not a purely subjective experience. Faith is based on the objective reality of who God is and what He has done. In fact, faith is based on a real Person and an historical event that's already taken place. The object of one's faith is Jesus Christ and His love expressed ultimately through His death on the cross. The *object* of your faith is what makes all the difference, not your faith in and of itself. Christian faith is faith in a Person. The more we come to know this Person – Jesus Christ – the more we trust Him. To know Him is to love Him, and we come to know Him even more by following and simply doing what He says. This is what separates Christianity from world religions. Christian faith is built on a relationship, not upon rules or religious activity.

At the heart of Christian faith is this truth: I do not get to know God, then do His will; I get to know Him *by* doing His will. This is why I must persevere in spiritual disciplines if I desire to grow in my faith (more on that in chapter 5).

Perhaps you're like so many I've talked to who have little *formal* spiritual background. You may not be at as much of a disadvantage as you think. In fact, in some cases, it's quite an advantage as we consider who God is and what He's like. Recent research from the Barna Research Group indicates that 76 million adults have not attended a religious service of any kind over the past six months.[12] To put this in perspective, the Boomers, the largest generation in American history, represent 77 million people. Clearly one-third of all adult Americans do not go to church at all. Barna notes this does not mean these people are not "religious." Most of them (62%) consider themselves "Christian" and are seeking to understand what they believe about God and their place in the world.

One man expressed to me what I think many people feel. He said he was certain there was a God but he didn't really know what to believe about this God. Therefore, he didn't know what to expect from God or how to approach Him. Perhaps you can relate. For many years surveys have consistently revealed that 90 to 95% or more of all Americans believe in "God." Numbers are generally 90% worldwide and between 60 to 80% in European countries. Supposedly 45% of all Americans attended a church service last Sunday, but I believe very few hold to a biblical perspective of God.

When I first met my wife, Stacy, we had a long-distance relationship. In fact, we did until we got married. The days we were together had long months between them. I couldn't wait to see her. And when we were together we didn't want to leave each other. The first time I picked her up at the airport we drove all the way to my parents' house holding hands. I loved being with her. I thought about her all the time. I would count the days when I would be with her again. Then we counted down to our wedding day! Finally, the big day arrived!

As we drove away for our honeymoon, she reached in the backseat and said, "Here, I've been waiting to give you this." She handed me a big three-ring binder. "Here's all the information you need to know about me, what I like and don't like, how you can make me happy, how to talk to me, what to say, and what not to say. You better start studying up or this marriage thing is going to get tough for you real fast."

Of course, this didn't really happen. But imagine if it did I'd say, "Wait a minute. This is not what I signed up for! What about the heart to heart, the sweaty palms, the passion, the yearning, the longing to be together, and the late-night conversations?" I'd say, "Stacy, I don't want to simply know *about* you; I want to know *you*. Simply put, I want you. You've missed the point."

Most people approach their spiritual life in the same way. Some think that's what a relationship with God looks like. They've never seen or experienced anything else. As a pastor I meet people all the time who are new to our church, or to any church. Most people fit into one of two categories: Either they're brand new to Christ and the whole idea of a forgiving God, or they're coming from a somewhat distorted understanding of God. It's interesting when I ask people about their spiritual journey. Those who've been in church for a long time will tell me all about their church experience. When I ask a new believer about his/her spiritual journey, you know what they talk about? Jesus. They talk about the forgiveness they've experienced, the freedom from sin, the burden lifted, the newfound joy and purpose in their lives. They tell me about their love for Jesus and do so with an excitement in their voice or a tear in their eye.

One lays out their resume of being a good club member, and the other talks about an exciting relationship with Someone who has saved his/her life. What happened? How did the "church person" turn what's supposed to be a vibrant, personal relationship into a list of evidences that prove they're a good club member? Somehow, over time we've made following Jesus about being a good church member. We've moved from being on mission with Jesus to being a member of an organization. You could say some moved from the heart to the head. You know a question that will stop a lot of church-going people in their tracks? "How would you describe your personal relationship with Jesus and how He's serving others through you in these days?" We can talk about church attendance or activities, but we stumble over a personal, ever-growing relationship with Jesus Christ. Have we missed the point?

In Philippians 3, Paul seeks to clear up the misconception that following Christ is like any other religion. He starts by laying out his spiritual resume. He says, If you want to talk about being religious, I'm your man. In fact, no one has been more religious than me. He says religious people put confidence in their ability to perform for God, and in so doing, they think they somehow gain His approval. He calls this "confidence in the flesh;" that is, in one's own religious efforts. In verse 4, he says that if anyone should have confidence in the flesh that he should have even more. But then he shares his new perspective.

Paul's great desire in life took on a dramatic shift after he experienced Christ's forgiveness. His great passion in life was not to find a church to his liking or simply become a good club member, pay his dues, and document how religious he was. He says, I've been there, done that. Instead, he had become so captivated, so transformed by the love of Christ, that the pursuit of Christ became the entire focus of his life. He didn't want to jump through any more religious hoops; trying to be good enough, "performing" for God. He now called it all "rubbish" (garbage, filth, dung). If that weren't enough, he goes further: "...I consider everything a loss compared to the surpassing greatness of knowing Christ Jesus my Lord, for whose sake I have lost all things." In fact, Paul had been pursuing Jesus so passionately and was coming to know Him so intimately, he was starting to think and act like Jesus. And like Jesus, he didn't even like religious people anymore. They were getting in the way of his new calling to live on mission with Jesus in the world.

Could it be that *you* have missed the point? Could it be that you've misunderstood what it means to follow Christ? Have you come to a point in your life that you pursue Jesus above all else? If you consider yourself a Christian, let me ask you, do you pursue Him daily, or has your Christian experience been relegated to "doing church"? There's a big difference.

Again, you may not have been indoctrinated into the church culture and so you've not been taught what it means to be a good club member. You don't carry around as much baggage as many others do. You're actually way ahead of those who've missed the point and spent their lives learning how to be really good club members, instead of passionate followers of Jesus.

Many people who have been church members much of their lives have turned Christianity into "churchianity." But when you get them alone and they get real honest, they'll tell you the whole club member approach has left them wanting. In fact, my guess is all of us know someone who's grown up in the church, been a good club member for years, and has left the church altogether. They simply decided to act on what they had been feeling for a long time; *it's just not worth it*. And it's not.

Now, there are varied reasons people get to this point, but the main reason is they were essentially told: *If you become a good club member, pay your dues, learn our songs, speak our language, and become like us – you'll find fulfillment in life*. And, with great hope, they bought it. They became a good club member and in the end realized, *This can't be all there is*. And they're right. Jesus promised us an "abundant life" (John 10:10). Why do we settle for less? Could it be that we really have missed the point of this wonderful, lifelong journey with Jesus? You've met people who have proven that it's possible to become a good church member and not become like Jesus. We've come to believe that if you become a member and if you're a member long enough, then you'll become like Jesus. We've missed the point.

What *is* the point? What should this journey of faith look like? Probably the smartest guy I've ever been around when it comes to spiritual growth and life is Dallas Willard. In his book, *Renovation of the Heart*, Willard says, "Spiritual formation is the Spirit-driven process of forming the inner world of the human self in such a way that it becomes like the inner being of Christ Himself."[13] I know that's a mouthful, but it basically comes down to this: It's an inside job before it becomes an outside job. Notice too that it is a process.

Many church people have never entered into that process. Somewhere along the way they reduced this Spirit-driven process to simply "going to a church." Way too many people have decided to come to meetings with a bunch of other club members who've missed the point. We don't need any more churches for church people. We have enough of those. We need churches for those who are far from God but long to know him and grow in Him. That's what Jesus wants us – the Church – to be. Then the Church becomes a movement again, not an institution.

There's another common misconception worth noting. The Bible is not the end in itself. So many Christians want to "go deeper" in the Word. In the end, what they mean is they want to learn more information. You can read the Bible and never become more like Jesus. Many Christians have committed themselves to a life of more and more knowledge and essentially leave Jesus completely out of the process. It's only through a humble heart, the power of God's Spirit, and the act of serving others that you are transformed to become like Him. Have we missed the point? Have you?

CHAPTER 8

Boarding the Wrong Plane

I recently crashed an AA meeting. I have a great love and respect for those in the recovering community. A good friend of mine was receiving his four-month coin and I was so proud of him, I wanted to be there to see him get it. The thing that attracts me to the recovering community is their raw, even unsettling, honesty. Expecting an explanation of one of the twelve steps or personal tirades of the irreligious, I heard stories of recovery, hope, and redemption instead. I thought I was going to a meeting, but what I got was, well, *church.* In fact, I experienced church in ways I typically don't *at* church. I experienced an uncommon honesty and an uncommon authenticity which brought forth an atmosphere of grace that most churches never experience.

I left wondering how can the church be more like an AA meeting? I knew the answer was found in what God had already told us to do. The entire atmosphere of the gathering seemed to breathe James 5:16 which says, "Therefore confess your sins to each other and pray for each other so that you may be healed. The prayer of a righteous man is powerful and effective." Perhaps you know that the first of the twelve steps is this: *We admitted we were powerless over our addiction - that our lives had become unmanageable.* It seems we've lost that sense of desperation in our lives these days. I've found that most view *church people* in one of two ways. Either they have it all together (because they never talk about their sin) or, more believable, they're hypocrites (because they sin like the rest of us but want us to think they don't). Have you come to a point in your life where you have admitted you're powerless to go on? You need to embrace this God who loves you more than you'll ever know. And if you haven't or wonder if you have, let me ask: How are you doing? How are you doing as the leader (lord) of your life? I'm guessing you're a really nice person, but I'm certain you're a lousy God. You need to realize that there is a power greater than yourself who can restore your sanity. He is the God of the Bible and He has come to us in Jesus.

If you don't get honest before God, admit that He's a lot bigger than you are, and embrace His love for you, you'll never get off that roller coaster of religion. And before some of you read on believing this doesn't apply to you, let me challenge you to think about this for moment. I've discovered that many Christians have simply "baptized" the world's system of performance and approval and brought it into their walk with God. Your heart resonates with the idea of a God who loves you for free and longs to take you just as you are, but the way you live betrays what you really believe.

You really think God will love you more if you please Him. You're motivated to follow Him to gain His approval (or, again, the approval of others). You find great worth in being so religious, so committed to Him. And you look down on those who are not as committed as you are. When you read the stories of the Bible, particularly the parables of Jesus, you think they're about someone else. You think the prodigal son is someone else. You think the lost sheep is about somebody else. You think the final hour worker called out to serve in the Master's vineyard is a story of someone else's life. You feel like you've been working faithfully since early in the morning and that you deserve a full day's wage.

You need to rediscover that the Bible really is about you. It's not that you were a sinner, you *are* a sinner. At every AA meeting each person introduces themselves by stating their name followed by "... and I am an alcoholic." Not, *I was* or *I used to be*, but *I am*. Perhaps we should all greet one another with *Hi, I'm 'so and so' and I am a sinner.*

You may be like some who have come to believe that grappling with these issues of faith is just not worth the time. Let me challenge you. This is the most important exercise you'll ever walk through. Discovering what really is at the core of life and at the core of what you believe about God is the most important journey you'll ever be on. In fact, throughout His ministry Jesus sought to put people in positions in which they had to decide to be for Him or against Him. He even said, "He who is not with me is against me, and he who does not gather with me scatters" (Matthew 12:30). Jesus was always very clear about His expectations and He wants you to decide, *Are you with me or not?* It's your choice. But beware; Jesus says that if you think you haven't yet decided, you already have.

For those of us who have decided to receive His forgiveness and are seeking to actually live forgiven, Jesus wants us to follow Him with all we've got or nothing at all. This is a sobering truth. He says He wants us to be either "hot or cold," not lukewarm (Revelation 3:15). Why does Jesus say this? Clearly He wants us to experience the life for which we've been created. But He also wants us to realize that if we choose to live apart from Him, it changes our entire existence. In fact, in the moment that we're living outside of His will we begin to live a kind of pseudo-life that we were never intended to live.

The stakes are higher than you could ever imagine, not only in the life to come, but in this life as well. If you've been waiting to respond to Jesus, I want you to think about the impact of your indecision. If you don't embrace the grace of God, it not only impacts the religious or spiritual aspect of your life, it impacts everything about your life.

Several years ago I was flying alone from Dallas to Houston. After a wild day of work I made a heroic effort to get to Love Field where I barely made it to the gate on time. I was whisked along with all the other passengers as we boarded the plane, and I sat down with a great sense of relief that I made it. Now I would let the pilot do all the work. I opened up a book and dove in for the short flight to Houston. Once in the air, the pilot offered the obligatory greeting, described our flight pattern, and estimated our time of arrival into Harlingen. Well into my book, I was barely listening, but I heard clearly that he said Harlingen and not Houston! I literally popped my head up and I think I said, "Oh no!" out loud. Immediately my mind raced through the last half hour. The gate number was the one for Houston. Even the sign at the gate indicated Houston. Surely they would not have allowed me to get on the wrong flight when I had a ticket to Houston! What seemed like an eternity was only a few moments when the pilot added, "I'm sorry. This plane will be arriving in Houston and then making its way on to Harlingen. I didn't mean to alarm anyone." Alarm anyone! My heart was still racing as I thought in an instant my whole evening had changed. Eager to join my family, I thought I was flying to the wrong destination.

For the rest of the flight I thought about what it would be like to board the wrong plane. Perhaps you have; a friend of mine once did. I thought about how I'd have to be re-routed to Houston on the next flight (if there was one at that time of night), or perhaps I'd have to arrive the next day.

But then I started to think about the implications of being on the wrong plane. My mind entered into a kind of *Twilight Zone* scenario. It would be bad enough to end up in the wrong destination, but that's not the only thing that would be wrong. Think about it, if you boarded the wrong plane, *everything* about your flight would be wrong. You would have the wrong pilot. The pilot that is supposed to be your pilot is flying the other plane. The seat you're in? That's the wrong seat! Your seat is on another plane. That drink? Those peanuts? They were not meant for you. Yours are on another plane. That flight attendant? That's not your flight attendant; she's on another plane. Those you spoke to while boarding, the person seated next to you, the sights you see outside your window, the clouds that go by... you're not supposed to experience any of it!

I began to think about the life that God has created us to live. He's called each of us to get on board His plane. He's called us to a life with Him; an adventure of grace. He is to be the pilot and we are to experience all that He has in store for us, but here's the truth about millions of people – they're on the wrong plane. It's bad enough that they are heading to the wrong destination, one for which they were not created, but they have the wrong pilot guiding them. Everything about their lives is wrong. They are not having the thoughts they were created to have. They are not seeing the things God has designed them to see. They are not encountering the people God has intended. They are not fulfilling their full potential for which they were created. They are not living out their place in his Kingdom. It's a sobering thought. Life without Christ means *everything* is wrong.

CHAPTER 9

Grace. Period.

B efore you think about *others* who might be on the wrong plane, remember it's quite possible to be on the right plane and still miss out on most of what God has designed you to experience. As I've stated, most Christians I know have not really embraced the grace of God available to them. They have come to believe that their Christian life is complete, precisely because they *have* boarded the right plane. *Once on board, I'm good. I'm home free.* What God offers as the beginning, they view as the end. They think, *I'm heading to the right destination and that's good enough for me.* It's possible to find your seat on "God's plane" (or in your pew in God's house) and never experience the life you were created to live.

I think millions of Christians are currently living that way. How else can we explain the graceless nature of many church-goers? What else would explain the "us against them" mentality among many, while Jesus taught us that it's actually "us *for* them?" How can we explain the magnet that many "anti" churches are for thousands of people? They are *anti* democrat, *anti* abortion, *anti* homosexual, *anti* liberal, or *anti* anything that doesn't match their view of how God works in the world, which is based on their own narrow experience.

Remember, for those on the wrong plane, everything is wrong. No wonder they think and act like they do. Scripture is clear: sinners sin because that's their job description. It's what they do. In fact, it's what we all do. The Bible would remind Christians and non-Christians alike that it is the one thing that binds us all together. "For all have sinned and fall short of the glory of God" (Romans 3:23).

Surely God is *anti* many things, but He's not *anti* people. He is *pro nobis* (for us). And "us" means all of us. Though a particular church may not be *for* the homosexual, God is. One's political views or view of the world may not match up biblically, but God is still *for* her or him. Jesus died to show that He is for us all. You've never met someone for whom Christ did not die.

Unfortunately, the church has not always been for those who were not on the right plane. Being on the right plane should set us free to love, forgive, and embrace others with the love of Christ – not push them away. It seems that many believers are sitting aboard a heaven-bound flight, looking out at those who are perishing. Some on board, disgusted by the sinner's ways, simply mock them and turn away repulsed as they go to hell. Maybe we really have forgotten why Jesus came. Maybe His Gospel really is simple. Perhaps it really is about one thing and one thing only.

It may sound as though I don't like the church. Actually, I *love* the church. I just don't like "church," I love the people of the church. I love the movement of God wherever that is expressed, I just don't like the institution that sometimes has very little to do with the movement of God in the world. The truth is I'm crazy about the church. I'm wild about the church I'm a part of, in particular. I see a church on mission with Jesus, seeking to restore the least and lost to Him. It just seems we need to rediscover the *one thing* we have to offer the world.

It seems in this age of pragmatic preaching we have tragically misplaced the Gospel of Grace. Many years ago, experts from around the world gathered in England for a conference on comparative religions. They were debating the unique, if any, contributions of Christianity to the world. After much debate, C.S. Lewis stepped into the room and when told what they were debating he said, "Oh, that's easy. It's grace."[14] The one thing Jesus came to bring us was grace. Period.

I've had the privilege of worshipping in churches all over the world. I've worshipped in the bush of Africa, in Hong Kong, Tokyo,

Manila, in the Philippines, and in Seoul, Korea. I've worshipped in places like Egypt, Israel, Amsterdam, Italy, Venezuela, Peru, Mexico, and Australia. Last year I spoke to a group of European pastors in Berlin, Germany – from the platform of our church in Texas via a live webcast. I've had the privilege of speaking in African-American churches, Asian churches, Hispanic churches, and European churches. I've been to great churches across the States from Brooklyn to Orange County. I'm excited about the church that is on mission in its various forms.

I love the Church universal, but I also love the local Church. I love each local expression of the Kingdom of God seeking to lead people to live on mission with Jesus in their corner of the world. Many of these churches have little in common, but the ones on mission with Jesus have one thing in common: the grace of God. Any group of people who seek to make a significant impact in their particular part of the world will do so by passionately communicating (and living out) the grace of God.

The Church I love the most is the Church Jesus envisioned. And the one He envisioned is the one that has one message, the Gospel of grace. It's the message of a God who seeks to restore and rebuild broken lives to His glory. The Church Jesus envisioned seeks to share that message in as many ways as possible, as many times as possible, through as many people as possible, to as many people as possible.

The Church Jesus envisioned is the Church that will stop at nothing to spread the grace of Christ to one person at a time until the whole world is touched by the love of God. It is the grace of God – His unmerited favor, His unconditional acceptance, His undeserved love – that compels the Church to do all that it does. There is no other message and no other motive. It's grace, period. The same is true in your own life. It's grace, period. God's grace gave you life. His grace got you out of bed this morning. His grace will give you your next breath, and His grace will lead you into eternity.

Is your life marked by grace, period? Would people describe you as a person of grace? If you would describe yourself as a Christian, consider this question: How does your life differ from a moral non-Christian? I know many moral non-Christian people. In fact, I know some non-Christian people who are actually more "moral" than some Christian people I know. Some are kinder, more loving, and more gracious. So, what is the one thing that would separate the Christian from others? Again, just one thing: grace. C.S. Lewis once said, "The Christian has a great advantage over other men, not by being less fallen than they, nor less doomed to live in a fallen world, but by knowing that he is a fallen man in a fallen world." Maybe that's where we all should start.

As I mentioned earlier, the one thing that ties us all together is that we're defined by our sin. If our problem was psychological, we would need a psychologist. If it were genetic, we would need a scientist. If it were financial, we would need an economist. But our problem is sin and we need a Savior.

That's the God you're looking for. He's really not who you think He is. He's bigger than you can comprehend. He's more powerful than your mind can grasp. He's more beautiful than you can imagine. And He loves you more than you can ever know. Believe me, God is not who you think He is.

Questions to ponder:

1. Do you think it's true that what a person believes about God is the most important thing about them? Why or why not?

2. Have you ever had a moment in which you felt "right-sized" before God? When was it and how would you describe your experience? How did it change your thinking?

3. Would you say that you have come to realize that faith is more about obedience and action than about beliefs and facts? If so, in what ways?

4. Would you say that you worship God simply for who He is, or do you worship Him for what He has done or is doing for you?

5. Would you say that your image of God has been marked by "snapshots" of grace and freedom or of legalism and religion? In what ways? What are some images of God that have left their mark on your life thus far? What pictures would you like to put in your personal "photo album" of God?

6. Have you ever felt like you're on the wrong plane? Do you feel that you may be even now?

Section Three
Grace Defined

"Man is born broken. He lives by mending. The grace of God is the glue."
Eugene O'Neill

CHAPTER 10

Why Jesus Came

If you put all that there is of the Christian faith (what it *really* is and what we've made it out to be) in a crucible and turned up the heat, one thing would remain: grace. In the end we have God, loving the world to Himself through Christ. All that's left is Jesus; His Person, His Heart, His Mission. As many people look at Christianity, or at least "Christendom," they're left dumbfounded by what they see. Casper the atheist was forced to ask, "Is this really what Jesus told you guys to do?"[15] Again, it seems possible to lose Jesus in a religion that now bears His name.

So far we've explored two big misconceptions that most of us have. One is about ourselves and the other is about God. Basically, the problem stated goes something like this: *I'm not who I think I am because God is not who I think He is, and what I think about God shapes what I think about myself.* We've explored some of the common struggles of identity that we all face in this life, and we've considered how our misconceptions of God impact who we are and how we live. In this section we'll look at what I've called the singular greatest word – better yet, truth or reality – you will ever know. *Grace* is defined as we look at why Christ came, what He did on the cross, why it matters so much, and how I can appropriate it into my life. This God of Creation, this God of the Bible that we've been pondering, is above all else the "God of grace."

Grace is a word we've used a lot already, but I'm certain that most of us have not fully grasped what it is. In this section I want you to come to grips with grace, to understand the essence of God's love for you, which is the beginning of a life forgiven. Whether you consider yourself a Christian or not I hope these pages will reveal to you, in greater clarity than ever before, what grace really is. After all, if it's not embraced for what it is, it will be something other than grace that captures you.

As we seek to define grace (and ultimately to be defined by it), we realize that like all great theological or philosophical truth, we must use analogy and story to grasp it. It is, after all, beyond our cognitive capabilities. Grace is not found in a well-crafted formula or diagramed thesis. As you will see, it's not ultimately found in a particular teaching or even some religious text. Grace is found in a Person. This is why I noted previously in the Introduction that the central teaching of Jesus was not some religious concept or set of rules but His *identity*. Grace is not found in religion; it is found in a Person. Let's first explore how and why grace came to us in Christ and then how we can encounter His grace and live in it. Put simply, let's see how the whole possibility of living forgiven came about.

The challenge with grace is that it's so rare and so seldom experienced in this life that many of us don't have a reference point. Let's start with two other words with which we may be more familiar – *justice* and *mercy*. Justice is getting exactly what you deserve. We traffic in justice throughout our lives. We like justice; at least when it's applied to someone else. If you do excellent work in school you get an A, if you do poorly in school you get an F. If you work hard for your employer for a particular period of time, you get a wage that you've earned. Anything less (or more) would not be what you deserve. If you do something wrong you deserve to be punished. That's *justice*. When we say someone is *just*, we're saying they are fair, impartial, honest, honorable, or even righteous. God is like that. He's always right. He never makes a wrong decision. He is fair and impartial in all His ways.

The other word, less familiar to us in our experience, is the word *mercy*. If justice is getting what you deserve then mercy is *not* getting what you deserve. If you do something wrong and do not receive punishment then you experience mercy. If you clearly break the law but the judge withholds the punishment you're due, it is an act of mercy. When we say that someone is merciful we mean that they are compassionate, kind, and forgiving. God is like that. He is merciful. He withholds punishment to those who deserve it.

God is surely the God of justice and mercy. He is always just and always merciful. For most of us it's hard to grasp how God can be both, so we live in one of the two extremes. Either He seems to always punish those who do wrong, or we think He would never punish anyone. To strike the balance and to truly get to the heart of God we must grasp the reality of grace. If justice is getting what we deserve and if mercy is not getting what we deserve, then grace *is* getting what we *don't* deserve. When someone extends grace to us, they are giving to us what we don't deserve to get. We receive good from them that is not based on our performance at all. In fact, an act of grace ceases to be grace if there are any ties to my particular behavior. Think about it, if someone else's response to me is based on anything I've done it becomes an act of either justice or mercy. This is why grace is so maddening and why so few truly grasp it. In a world where the score is kept and where performance and approval count, grace is about not keeping score and about not counting at all.

I remember sitting at a wedding rehearsal dinner beside a young woman who was working on her doctorate in math. Of course, as an art major, I was impressed. I said, "Wow, that's amazing, I've never been too good with numbers." She responded, matter-of-factly, "Oh, we don't really use numbers anymore." Huh? Have you ever been in a conversation and suddenly realized that you had no idea what the person was talking about? I didn't even know how to respond. Math without numbers? That's like astronomy without stars or zoology without animals, isn't it? Apparently you reach a certain point in mathematics where numbers become elementary, child's play.

That's the way God's love is. It's what Philip Yancey calls the "new math of grace."[16] There's a point in our relationship with God that we move to a whole new level of understanding and intimacy called "grace," where religion becomes elementary – child's play – to the person truly seeking the heart of God. Grace is math without numbers. It is a place where His grace reigns and where you stop counting. You no longer need to keep score when you enter the kingdom of God. You stop counting rights and wrongs in your life and in the lives of others around you. It is a life where grace alone matters and where grace drives everything you do. This is the life into which God is calling you. Before we get to how we can live in this grace every day, let's explore how it came to be.

Years ago I heard a story credited to Billy Graham about the time he was walking along with his young son, Franklin. They came upon an ant pile that had been disrupted, and the ants were bustling around in a frenzy of activity (apparently they start rebuilding their home immediately). His son was troubled by the near destruction of the ant pile and wanted to help the tiny ants somehow. The wise father took advantage of a teaching moment to reveal a deep theological truth to his son. Allow me to embellish and offer my own version of the story.

Imagine that you and I come upon this ant pile and we decide, *Let's help them. After all, we're so much smarter and so much bigger than they are.* We get down on our knees and start pushing the scattered, fine dirt together with our hands. Of course, soon we're covered with ants, stung multiple times, and done with that strategy in no time. We realize quickly that the only way we can really help them is to somehow communicate with them. We bend over the mound and begin yelling at the pile of activity. "Hey, ants! We're just a couple of humans and we're here to help you. Listen up!" The flurry of activity continues without any recognition of our existence. Some parallels to our existence and denial of a Deity start to emerge.

Clearly the only way to communicate to these tiny ants is to get down on their level, enter into their world, even become one of them. I bust out my human shrinking machine (I know, work with me). You and I enter the machine and push the "ant" button and suddenly – ZAP – we're not only ant sized but we look like ants! We walk, talk, and smell like ants. We walk into Antville and tell the crowd that we have come from far away to help them. We announce that we know we look like ants, we sound like ants, but we're actually humans. The ants look at one another dumbfounded.

"What's a human?" I hear one whisper to another. "Are these guys crazy?" another asks. We continue on, "We look like ants, but I promise we're humans. We are actually much bigger than you and, no offense, but much smarter. There's a whole world out there, and you guys have not even begun to imagine how big it is. Anyway, we're here to help."

Finally, one wise, elderly ant (okay, so most ants live about a year) stands up (do they ever sit down?) and says, "Ah yes. I believe in humans. My grandfather once told of seeing the bottom of a human's foot long ago. He said that humans are so large that we cannot fathom how big they are."

All the other ants now think the great wise ant is crazy too. As we try to defend ourselves and explain the world from which we come, soon enough all the ants think we're nuts and throw us into ant prison. Ultimately, as we continue to try and describe our former selves – who we *really* are – and our reasons for coming to their world, they decide they don't want to hear it any more. It is too far-fetched, too disturbing to their already neatly defined existence. They would have to rethink everything, rewrite history, and reconsider their place in the world. Maybe they're not the center of it after all. Finally, they decide to rid their ant pile of both of us, and we're sentenced to die. Our coming was too much for them to handle, and they just couldn't deal with it. It would, in the end, require way too much change.

Of course, this story of the humans who became ants pales in comparison to the story of the God who became a man. But tell me, how else could He communicate to us but to become one of us? For those in Jesus' day, like many in our day, it's just too much to handle. Their well-formed theology and concise worldview would not allow them to accept a God so approachable, so personal, so real. They would have to change everything. Their god was neat, boxed in, even safe. They had figured him out; or so they thought.

The same is true today. Most theists would agree with the cry of every Muslim: "God is great!" Surely He is, but no supernatural being was needed to tell us that. But that God is small, that He has become one of us and that we can know Him, this is the truth that Jesus alone has come to reveal to us. People ask me, "How do you know there is a God?" My quick answer is He came here and told us so! Poet John Donne wrote, "Twas much, that man was made like God before, but that God should be like man... much more." When God wanted to show the world how much He loves us, He sent His Son to us. God shows His love "in Person." Love starts with God and to show us what love is, He sends Jesus. 1 John 4:9 says, "This is how God showed His love among us: He sent His One and Only Son into the world that we might live through Him." This is why Jesus came and much more. Read on.

CHAPTER 11

What Really Happened on the Cross?

A few human beings know, in the moment, that they're about to die. I've talked to people in that moment. I've watched people die. *TIME* Magazine did an essay noting it's almost instinctive that, in that moment, people want to send a message. They want someone to know their story. A brotherhood of miners, trapped beneath the earth's surface, scrawl messages on a wall in their final hours. Russian crewmen in a sunken submarine write notes to loved ones in a last-minute, air-deprived struggle for life. Passengers on a JAL airliner write notes to loved ones while spiraling to their deaths. Prisoners of the Nazis in a Warsaw ghetto, after seeing everyone else either shot or starved to death, took their last breaths to write notes and stored them in the crevasses of the walls hoping someone other than the Nazis would find them and read their stories.

On September 11, 2001, many cell phone calls were made to offer final words to loved ones. In that final moment, all the scaffolding of life gets stripped away. All the tired goals we spend our lives chasing – success, reputation, security, wealth, comfort, ease – mean nothing. A person is left with what they really believe, what they really want to build their lives on. We spend much of our lives pretending that it won't, but that moment will come for each of us. If that moment were to come to you right now, what would you write? What would you say? What's the message you really want to tell? What's your story so far? What do you want it to be?

On a Friday afternoon just outside of Jerusalem, that moment came to a young rabbi being crucified for claiming to be God in the flesh. Oddly enough, the reality of His death had actually come to Him long before this moment. In John 18 (when He was arrested), it says, "Jesus, knowing all that was going to happen to Him, went out and asked, "Who is it you want?" (vs. 4). Paul would tell us later that God had actually planned this moment "before the creation of the world" (Ephesians 1:4). The apostle Peter says, "He was chosen before the creation of the world" (1 Peter 1:20). Death was imminent on the cross, and Jesus knew it. He had only moments to live and in His final words, we hear His story. His last words are of supreme importance to us, because they express the cry of His heart at this critical moment in history. The cross would be His final pulpit, and from it He would preach His final sermon. It would be, at once, His longest and shortest sermon, lasting six hours and containing only a few short phrases.

If you want to live forgiven you must fully grasp what took place on the cross. And the key to unlocking the mystery of the cross is to consider the most perplexing, uncomfortable, and difficult words that ever came from the lips of Jesus. In His final moments on the cross, He cried out, "My God, my God, why have you forsaken me?" (Matthew 27: 46). He's actually quoting Psalm 22:1, but clearly this is a cry of anguish. I've had many people ask me if I really believed the Father had abandoned Him? Could it be that God the Father really did forsake Him?

Many theologians say there's no way God the Father would have abandoned or turned His back on His Son. To understand the difficulty of these words we must first understand the nature of the Triune God. The Trinity (Father, Son, and the Holy Spirit) is at the core of biblical Christianity. It's important to note that the Trinity is a relationship of submission. The Son says He does nothing apart from "the Father's initiative" and that He does only what He sees the Father doing. Jesus says that ultimately the Spirit would come and "will guide you in all truth." At Jesus' baptism the Father says, "This is my beloved Son." In John 17:11, Jesus prays for the Father to make His followers "one even as we are one." Could it be that for the first time in all of history there was violence done, not only to

Jesus, but to the Trinitarian relationship of the Father, Son, and Holy Spirit? Understood correctly, this cry of anguish found in Matthew 27 is one of the most powerful, perplexing, and comforting words that Jesus ever spoke to us. In fact, I pray that as we unpack them you will be overwhelmed, besieged, and undone by God's love for you.

In an attempt to understand more fully what Jesus meant, we need to go back to the Garden of Gethsemane the night before the cross. How could Judas have betrayed his Master? Could he not see what was coming? How could the crowd, on what we call Palm Sunday, exalt Jesus with shouts of praise and within a week (by Friday) shout curses instead, demanding that He be crucified? With such a throng throwing themselves at His feet one week, how did Jesus get arrested and killed the next? As I read the Gospel accounts of the final week of Jesus' life I see undercurrents that explain the shift. But through it all, I'm struck with the reality that Jesus is in complete control of all that is happening. If you look carefully and listen to His words, it seems as though He Himself is writing the script. As the story unfolds, you realize that's precisely what's happening. He has a secret ambition. The dramatic shift takes place in the Garden of Gethsemane where Jesus is arrested. It's interesting to note that just prior to His arrest John 18:4 says that Jesus knew "all things that were to happen to Him."

One may ask if He knew all things that were to happen, did He have a choice? There's a difference between foreknowledge and predetermined events. Jesus went to the cross because He saw our sin and subsequent separation from God. In a word, He went to the cross because He saw *you and me.*

Matthew's account of the events leading up to the moment of Judas' betrayal is the most descriptive account of all that Jesus was going through. After Judas agrees to betray Him Jesus shares the Passover meal with His disciples. During the meal Jesus tells Peter that he will deny Him three times that night. From the Upper Room in Jerusalem, stuffy with the smells of lamb, bitter herbs, and sweaty bodies, Jesus and the eleven disciples head for the cool, spacious olive grove of the garden called Gethsemane. Spring is in full bloom at the time of the Passover, the night air was fragrant with blossoms.

Emotionally drained (Luke 22:45 tells us that they were "exhausted from sorrow), the disciples reclined under the moon and stars of a now peaceful night and quickly drifted off to sleep. Jesus, however, would find *no* peace, *no* rest at all. Matthew says He "began to be sorrowful and troubled" (26:38). Mark adds that He was "deeply distressed." Often Jesus would go off alone, most of the time to *be alone*, but on this night He would need His best friends there with Him. Jesus the Man needed human companionship. Solitary confinement is the worst form of punishment our species has ever devised, and in this moment Jesus didn't want it.

When His disciples failed Him, Jesus did not try to conceal His hurt: "Could you not keep watch for one hour?" (Matthew 22:40). His words suggest something more ominous than loneliness. Is it possible that for the first time ever He did not want to be alone with the Father? A great struggle is under way in the heart of Jesus. No formal, well recited prayers would come on this night. No poetic, nicely phrased petitions in these prayers. Dr. Luke tells us "being in anguish, He prayed more earnestly, and His sweat was like drops of blood falling on the ground" (Luke 22:44). He describes a rare medical condition that had taken effect known as "hematidrosis," in which the blood vessels, under such stress, expand and burst into the sweat glands. Imagine what happens next: He falls face down on the ground crying out to God the Father.

Why was Jesus in such agony? I would suggest that you and I have never known this kind of anguish. I've talked to many people who knew they had only days, even hours, to live. Some are terrified but most are accepting, even calm. Jesus seems anything but calm. Knowing what was to come, was He afraid of the beatings, the scourging, the spikes driven through His wrists and feet? Was it the fear of death that tortured Him so? Here we realize that sometimes it's a blessing *not* to know the future. Was it the betrayal of His closest friends? Was it the denial of Peter? Was it a combination of all of these things together? No. I believe that the pain Jesus knew in the garden and would experience on the cross was greater than any one of those things and even greater than all of those things combined.

To know what was at the heart of His agony, we must understand what He meant when He referred to the "cup" the night before in the Garden. In Matthew 26:39, Jesus cries out, "My Father, if it is possible, may this cup be taken away from me. Yet not as I will but as you will." There has been much confusion as theologians have pondered the meaning of the "cup" along with, I think, misunderstanding of what Jesus meant by the "cup."

What was this cup? What was Jesus hoping to avoid? It was not merely death. It was not physical pain on the cross. It was not the scourging or humiliation. It was not the torture of nails being driven through His body, not the horrible thirst, nor was it the disgrace of being spat upon or beaten. Again, it was not even *all* these things combined. I say this because those were all the things Jesus said *not* to fear. In Luke 12:4-5, He said, "And I say to you my friends, do not be afraid of those who kill the body, and after that have no more they can do." "But," He went on to add, "I will show you whom you should fear: Fear Him who, after He has killed, has power to cast you into hell; yes, I say to you, fear Him!" Clearly, what Christ dreaded most about the cross was *not* physical death. It was the outpouring of the wrath He would endure from His Holy Father. Again, the key here is a clear understanding of the "cup."

The cup was a well-known Old Testament symbol of the divine wrath of God against sin. Isaiah 51:17 says, "Awake, awake! Stand up, O Jerusalem, You have drunk at the hand of the Lord the cup of His fury; you have drunk the dregs of the cup of trembling, and drained it out." In Jeremiah 25:15-16, the Lord tells the prophet, "Take this *cup* of fury from my hand, and cause all the nations, to whom I send you, to drink it. When they drink it, they will stagger and go mad because of the sword I will send among them." He goes on to add, "Drink, be drunk, and vomit! Fall down and rise no more, because of the sword which I will send among you" (Jeremiah 25:27). Pretty graphic stuff. What Jesus was experiencing on the cross was nothing less than the cup of the terrible wrath of God! It's worth noting here that *wrath* is not an out-of-control reaction of someone going "postal" on an angry rampage. God is beyond that. Wrath is God's holy reaction to sin and in this case, it is unleashed on the Son. The cup that Jesus was to drink was the vile, repulsive cup of sin bringing upon Him the full fury of the wrath of God.

I can still remember a moment in middle school when I came upon a fight in the hallway. One kid was wearing out another, fists on face. I can still remember the sound of the one bully's fist hitting the other kid over and over again. I can see the blood coming down his face and splashing on the linoleum floor. I remember thinking, "I don't know what he did but I don't think he deserves *this*." Before any of us had time to do anything a teacher was there to stop the madness. Even as I write this I get that same sickening feeling I had that day. It's a feeling that goes beyond the sight of blood or watching violence played out before you. It's that grotesque sense of extreme injustice, of utter helplessness, and of a rage so strong that once unleashed it becomes not only inhuman, but clearly un-human. If you've ever seen anything like that or perhaps (forgive me), have ever experienced something like that, you cringe at the thought of it.

Now, consider this: The One who had never tasted the tiniest drop of sin, the One who had never been separated from the Trinitarian relationship, will now bear the full brunt of the divine fury of God upon the most terrible, grotesque sins ever committed by every person who would ever live. This, of course, includes *your* sins.

2 Corinthians 5:21 says, "He made Him who knew *no* sin to become sin for us, so that we might become the righteousness of God in Him" (more on this verse later in this section). That holy transaction of our sins being poured into Him, the full wrath of God unleashed upon the Son, is what Jesus feared most. He had never been separated from the Father until the cross. God the Father has never abandoned anyone except His own Son.

This is the *only* way to explain the perplexing prayer of Jesus on the cross: "My God, My God, why have you forsaken Me?" (Matthew 27:46). Friend, as you read this, do you realize what you've been saved from? God imputed (transferred, exchanged, ascribed) *your* sin to Christ and then punished *Him* for it. Peter puts it this way: "He Himself bore our sins in His body on the tree, so that we might die to sins and live for righteousness; by His wounds you have been healed" (1 Peter 2:24). Don't you feel a need to stop right now and thank Him? Go ahead and do it.

In the garden we find the only place where Jesus addresses God as *My Father* (Matthew 26:39, 42). In fact, Mark records He prayed, "Abba, Father." *Abba* is the Aramaic equivalent of "Daddy" or "Dada." I believe that Jesus was experiencing a kind of "holy separation anxiety." What parent has not seen the terror in the eyes of a child while being left behind – as if their eyes and their cry was saying, *I can't believe that you are leaving me!* or *Why have you abandoned me?!* I believe that is precisely what Jesus went through on the cross, and the garden was a prelude to the pain He knew was coming. With this cry He yelled, "My *God...*" not "My Father" (the only place He does this). Did the Father really abandon the Son? Was there really violence done to the Trinity while Jesus was on the cross!? I can't explain it theologically or understand it rationally, but how else can you justify this cry of Jesus?

As He cried out in anguish, God's inflexible holiness and boundless love collided, and our redemption was made possible. That's what happened on the cross. For you to be fully forgiven, Jesus *had* to be fully abandoned. In that moment, the Man Jesus was not in charge, the Father was. What does this transaction over 2,000 years ago have to do with you today? Everything. It is more relevant than today's newspaper and more powerful than any truth you'll ever know. "You are forgiven," He says. Jesus, the Lamb of God, took on the full fury of God's wrath. He died so that you wouldn't have to, and now you can live forgiven.

Let me ask you a question that I think is vital to your understanding of why Jesus came and what it means to be a Christian. In the previous paragraphs we explored exactly what happened on the cross. Let's consider a question I hear often: *Why did Jesus have to die?* I had a woman recently say to me, "It seems so severe." What she meant was that she felt the intensity of Christ's punishment on the cross was too extreme, even gratuitous.

I heard these same thoughts several years ago following the movie, *The Passion of the Christ*. One man asked, *Why was so much time given to the punishment of Jesus in the film?* I remember thinking myself that the scourging scene seemed to go on forever.

Could it be that God takes sin more seriously than I do? And could it be that the severity of Christ's suffering was necessary in order to provide forgiveness to the most heinous of all sins committed by all of humankind?

The question may not be why did Jesus have to die, but why such a horrific death? Of course, the quick answer that many Christians would bring is *because of our sin* or *to save us from hell* and most of us end there. Again, did Jesus come to save us from the penalty of sin or is there still more to what He did on the cross? I'm writing this book because I think there's a big difference between *being* forgiven and actually *living* forgiven. Or perhaps they are two wings of a single airplane, two horses pulling the same wagon, or two realities that define what it means to be a "Christian." The book of James would tell us that the latter is evidence of the former. Faith (receiving forgiveness) without action (living forgiven) is no faith at all. Could it be that being a Christian is not what we think it is?

CHAPTER 12

What it Means to be a "Christian"

A s a Christian, and particularly as a Christian leader, I wish we had another name. "Christian" has been so abused, misused, and maligned. Once upon a time a Christian was a disciple (an apprentice, a learner, a "copy-cat") of Jesus. Today, around the world, "Christian" has about the same identification as words like *American, European, Muslim,* or *Conservative.* I think, like so many of my contemporaries, I love being identified with Christ but not so much with Christianity as it is seen and understood in our current culture. I suppose I'm just a "Jesus person." That's what I want to be.

In the beginning of his classic book, *The Normal Christian Life,* Watchman Nee poses the question, "What is the normal Christian life?"[17] He suggests that a study of the Scripture, particularly passages like the Sermon on the Mount, "should lead us to ask whether such a life has in fact ever been lived upon the earth, *save only by the Son of God Himself.* But in that last clause lies immediately the answer to our question." Clearly Jesus is our model for the Christian life. In fact, the word "Christian" literally means, "little Christ." I suppose we could just call it the "Christ life" or the "Jesus life." But this is not to say that living the Jesus life is simply following His way of life or using His life as a model for living. True, to live like Jesus means to live a life that looks comprehensively like His, but authentic Christianity is more than that. In fact, something must happen from the inside out or a person will never be a Christian. You don't follow a set of rules or laws as, say, a Muslim or a Jew and then call yourself a Christian.

It's rare to find a person who actually lives fully forgiven. As a result, few of us have really seen authentic Christianity. I want you to read this passage below from the book of Romans. I mentioned earlier that every person, whether he or she realizes it, is a theologian. If you have never read from the book of Romans, you're about to read a portion of what many have called the greatest theological document ever written. It will help you unpack what it really means to be a Christian in the context of the three words we explored earlier – *justice, mercy,* and *grace*. Paul has just pointed out that there is no way we can get to God through religion, which he often refers to as "the law." He has pointed out in Romans 3:10 that "there is no one righteous, not even one; there is no one who understands, no one who seeks God." He doesn't sound too optimistic about our ability to get to God through our own efforts. In this context, read the passage carefully, meditatively:

> *"But now a righteousness from God, apart from law, has been made known, to which the Law and the Prophets testify. This righteousness from God comes through faith in Jesus Christ to all who believe. There is no difference, for all have sinned and fall short of the glory of God, and are justified freely by His grace through the redemption that came by Christ Jesus. God presented Him as a sacrifice of atonement, through faith in His blood. He did this to demonstrate His justice, because in His forbearance He had left the sins committed beforehand unpunished – He did it to demonstrate His justice at the present time, so as to be just and the One who justifies those who have faith in Jesus." (Romans 3:21-26)*

This passage is loaded with theological significance. In it we see there is a righteousness that has come to us apart from religion. In fact, it's a righteousness that comes to us that has nothing to do with religion. Whoa, that's good news! There is no difference between the religious and non-religious, the sinner and the "saint." We're all in the same boat; namely, a sinking one. Then Paul dives into these powerful concepts of justice, mercy, and grace. Simply put, he says:

- **In His *justice* God demanded payment.**

Verse 23 says that we have all fallen short of God's standard. All of us have sinned. If God were to simply overlook our sin He would cease to be just. In verse 26, it says that God sent Jesus to demonstrate His justice. Sin demands payment, so Jesus came to take on the payment of our sin.

- **In His *mercy* God delayed payment.**

Verse 25 says that because of His "forbearance" (His patient mercy), He left sins unpunished. As the Law was presented, we came to understand the nature of God (namely, His righteousness) and it became clear that we could not measure up to His holiness.

- **In His *grace* God delivered payment.**

Verse 24 says we are "justified" (made right), "by His grace." The grace was made possible "through the redemption that came by Jesus Christ." God presented Him as "a sacrifice of atonement." Atonement literally means payment or penance, that which is rightfully due. A perfect, satisfying, complete payment was necessary, and God delivered this payment for our sins through the sacrifice of Jesus – the *only* perfect sacrifice.

Again, let me offer a story to convey one of the deepest theological truths known to man. Imagine that you and I are friends and that I show up at your house on your sixteenth birthday. Much to your surprise, your father has given you a brand-new car! But it's not just a car, it's a small, super-fast sports car. (Okay, so your dad may be loving but not too smart.) Anyway, you want to check out how it drives, so you and I jump in to take it for a spin. We're cruising around town and you decide to see what this baby's got under the hood. You take it from zero to sixty in no time and we're both amazed at the power of the engine. Right about the time we're high-fiving each other you look in the rearview mirror and see the flashing lights of a police car behind us. Uh oh, not a good way to begin your first day of driving – in your new car!

The officer asks why you're driving so fast and you look at your brand-new car, thinking it's obvious. He gives you a ticket, noting that you were in a school zone doing sixty. You realize that if you can't come up with $600, you'll need to report before a judge the next Monday. Do you know a sixteen-year-old with $600 lying around? You show up at the courtroom early on Monday. As the judge enters, you are thrilled to see that the presiding judge is none other than… your dad! You have two thoughts: This is the dad who loves you so much he gave you a car for your sixteenth birthday! This is also the dad who is a by-the-book kind of judge. He follows every detail of the law and is known to be strict but always fair. "Uh oh, what will he do?" you wonder. Will his adherence to the law or his love for you prevail? Put another way, which will triumph, justice or love?

With a serious and stern voice he asks, "How do you plea?" You sigh. This is not a good start. "Guilty," you say ashamedly. "What's that, I didn't hear you?" your dad asks loudly. "Guilty, sir." "Do you understand the punishment for this offense?" "Yes, sir." "Do you understand that if you cannot come up with the payment that you will go to jail?" You think, "Dad, where's the love? This is my first offense. A little… what's it called…grace?"

Your father announces that according to the law there are only two options: Pay the price according to the law or go to prison. There are no other options. You realize you're doomed. Sixteen years old and you're heading to the big house. Just then, your dad does some-thing that you could have never anticipated. He stands up, takes off his black robe, and steps down from his bench. He walks over to the court clerk and pulls out six, fresh $100 bills. As he hands them over to her, he counts them out loud, "… four hundred, five hundred, six hundred." You sit in amazement with your mouth open. You dad walks back to his bench, puts his robe back on, and sits down. He hits his gavel and announces, "Your payment has been made; you are now free to go."

In that moment, what would you do? You could decide that you are unworthy to receive such a gift (and you would be right), and you could refuse the payment and go to jail. You could realize that the love of your father has won the day, and he would want nothing more than for you to receive his payment for your "sin." What would you do? Of course, this is exactly what God has done for you in Christ. You and I have been caught dead guilty in our sin. There is no denying it. We've been caught and according to the "Law" we deserve to go to hell and pay the price for our sins. Just as there are physical laws that govern the physical universe, there are spiritual laws that govern our relationship with God. There is right and wrong and there is justice. There is a price to be paid for sin. But, as we've noted, there is also *grace*.

Our loving Father, the righteous Judge, has stepped down from His throne in heaven and has paid the price for our sin through Christ's sacrifice on the cross. You and I are now faced with a decision. We can either say, *Nah, I'll just pay the price myself* (even though we can't), or we can simply receive the greatest gift ever offered to us. God wants you to be set free and not have to pay the horrible price for your sin.

I shared this with a young man not long ago and asked him what he would do now that he understood what Christ had done for him. He said, "I can't receive that." When I asked, "Why not?" he explained that he didn't feel worthy; he had not earned that kind of forgiveness. At first blush this sounds rather humble, but underneath this kind of thinking is actually extreme pride. He would not accept God's love, because it didn't put him in the driver's seat. He wanted to *do* something to warrant this kind of forgiveness so that he could forever know that he deserved it. He wanted to be the one worthy of this kind of love. Who said we were worthy? That's the whole point. God has gone to great lengths to show that we are unworthy. More correctly, *we* have gone to great lengths to show ourselves unworthy.

I feel the need to pause for a moment and address something with which a growing number of people seem to struggle. I recently talked to a man who wondered if he really needed to be forgiven at all. As a student of our culture and particularly of the spiritual condition of our culture, I like to explore emerging faith trends and consider why they've taken place and what impact they might have.

For years there has been much talk about the downward spiral of morality and the breakdown of any real sense of what is right and what is wrong. What many see as the disintegration of truth in our culture forces us to ask what's going on? Some people answer this question with no reference to God, the Bible, Jesus, or even morality. They enter into conversations and debates about education, economy, the media, and government, among other culprits. Again, we tend to eliminate the answers before we even start asking the questions. It seems that we have collectively shifted away from God and His Word, and having been so blessed by God, we've turned then to ourselves believing that our blessings were somehow our own doing. "Pride comes before the fall," the Bible says, and it seems apparent we're on our way down. Unless there's a significant shift in our culture, a shift that I think can still happen, we'll continue to see this move away from the foundations that have held us for so long.

However, I believe that many Christian leaders are confused today, and I think many are fighting the wrong battle. The battle in our culture (often referred to as the "culture war") is not a battle over *truth* as much as it is a battle over *grace*. No doubt we need to teach the truth, live by the truth, and know the Truth. But Christians will never win our culture by arguing that we are right and "they" are wrong. We will win the battle when we decide, as Jesus showed us, that ultimately this is a battle of love. And as Christ showed us, love will always prevail.

This is an important concept to grasp: The Law (religion) will not save us, not because it is evil but because it is *incomplete*. Jesus Himself said, "Do not think that I have come to abolish the Law or the Prophets; I have not come to abolish them but to fulfill them" (Matthew 5:17). The Law showed us the nature of God and His standards, and it showed us that we could never meet His standards.

The Law is like a mirror. Imagine you wake up with a serious case of bed head. If you don't do something before you leave the house you're going to have, not just a *bad* hair day, but the *worst* hair day. You know this because the mirror has revealed it to you. But you don't pull the mirror off the wall and try to comb your hair with it. The mirror is designed to *show* you the problem, not *fix* the problem. The same is true with the Law or any religion. Our own efforts to get to God simply reveal that we can't get to Him. The Law is incomplete. Only in Christ do you find the completion, the fulfillment of the Law. Dwight L. Moody once said, "The Law tells me how crooked I am. Grace comes along and straightens me out."

Clearly, Christ has done what we couldn't do. We are all sinners. This is what separates Christianity from all other religions of the world. In fact, it's why I say that Christianity is not a religion at all. Years ago I heard Bill Hybels of Willow Creek Community Church in Chicago, explain the simple difference between religion and Christianity this way:

Religion is spelled "D-O;" Christianity is spelled "D-O-N-E."

Religion is all about what I must do to appease a holy God who demands that I be like Him. Think about it. If God is holy, how good would you have to be to get to Him? The Bible says we would have to be perfect, and even then we would fall short. As noted in the previous chapter, religions around the world are all about what we must *do* to get to God. Religion will never get us to God.

Christianity is based solely on what Christ has already *done* for us. He died on the cross for our sins so that we wouldn't have to die. He set us free from sin so that we could live in the freedom of being forgiven. He's done all that needs to be done – game over. You simply need to receive the gift of His grace made possible for you through His death on the cross. As we'll see in Section Five, the completed work of Christ on the cross doesn't mean that *I'm* done; it means that I have a new start on a new trajectory toward a new life. This is the Jesus life, life in the kingdom of God, a life forgiven. "Done" refers to His work done for me, not my work done for Him. It means that I am forgiven and now seek to live forgiven.

Do you believe that "all have sinned and fallen short of the glory of God" (Romans 3:23)? Have you not proven throughout your life that "all" includes *you*? I know I have. The cross alone offers the solution for your old sin nature. You were created for God, not for yourself. Why? Because God wants to love you and He wants you to experience His love. It's His nature; it's His character. In fact, He *is* love.

This indescribable God created us to have an eternal relationship with Him. And He creates us in time and space and then puts us in the perfect environment in which to choose to love Him or not. Listen to that again: In all the ways God could have created us, He created us for eternity – not for a brief time on this earth. His whole purpose in creating us is so that we might be loved by Him, respond by loving Him, and worship Him not for time alone but for eternity. Why the "now" then? Why this pit stop on earth for 80 to 90 years or so? In part, so that we would choose to love Him. As I've noted, without choice there is no love, so God gives us this unspeakable gift, the opportunity (for a time) to decide whether or not to give Him our lives.

So to be a Christian is to live in a personal relationship with Jesus Christ. It means that you have decided to let Him be Lord, Ruler, Leader, of your life. In light of all of this, would you describe yourself as a "Christian?" It would be good to stop here and consider the most important decision you'll ever make in your life. I hope as you have read to this point that you have come to understand why Jesus came and what He's done for you. I've gone to great lengths in this chapter to help you realize what Christ accomplished on the cross and why it matters so much to you and me personally. I want you to read the next few pages carefully and consider whether or not you've ever truly received the grace of God as your own. And I want to give you a chance to decide for yourself to live forgiven.

As each of us must decide how we will respond to what Christ has done, I want to offer a word to the skeptic. First, I'm glad you're still with me. You've endured much to this point. But I want to encourage you to consider your life as it is. That is, consider your present philosophy of life, your current way of living. As you examine this new way of life I want to ask you to consider a real, if not scary, possibility. Proverbs 14:12 says, "There is a way that seems right to a man, but in the end it leads to death." The intriguing thing about this verse is not that the way leads to death but that it seems so right.

I have to ask you what might be a life-altering question: Could it be that you've been going the wrong way? Might you be on the wrong plane? Jesus said, "I am the Way, the Truth, and the Life. No one comes to the Father but through me" John 14:6. Say what you will about Christianity or the Church in its present form, the language of Jesus is clear: "I am the singular, One and Only Way." Implied here and in Proverbs is this: There are other ways that seem right but none of them will lead to life. In fact, as noted, they lead to death.

Could it be that it's time for you to step across a line of faith, to cross a bridge from your current life to the Jesus life, from a life unforgiven to a life forgiven.

How can I be forgiven?

• **Admit that you need to *be* forgiven.**

   Just say, "God, I'm sorry…" Admitting that you need forgiveness is to admit that "*all* have sinned and fall short of the glory of God" (Romans 3:23), and that "all" includes you. If you've never done this, just admit to God that you need forgiveness.

• **Believe that Jesus died on the cross to take your punishment and that He rose again, conquering death and hell, for you.**

   This is going to require that crazy thing called faith. Faith is believing in that which you cannot see, or perhaps cannot fully understand. Remember, faith precedes reason, so *as* you believe you open the door to understanding. You may be wondering how this faith can be expressed. Do you just close your eyes as if wishing on a star? (Dorothy in the Wizard of Oz, wanting to go back to Kansas comes to mind.) One way to express your faith is by putting words to it. Paul offers these words. Offer them as your own. He says, "… if you confess with your mouth, 'Jesus is Lord,' and believe in your heart that God raised Him from the dead, you will be saved" (Romans 10:9). Allow Him to be your Savior (*Forgiver*), that is to say that He died to save you from sin and death. He died to set you free to live forgiven. Let Him be Lord; He will now be the *Leader* of your life. Receive Him right now. The Bible says, "...to all who received Him, to those who believed in His name, He gave the right to become children of God" (John 1:12). Everyone has been created by God, but only those who have "received Him" are called His children.

- **Commit your life to Him and decide to live forgiven.**

Become His disciple and live for Him. You have been forgiven so that you might live forgiven. Jesus Himself said, "...If anyone would come after me, he must deny himself and take up his cross daily and follow me" (Luke 9:23). If you have truly grasped God's great love for you, seen most notably on the cross, then this becomes the only response. He deserves your life. Offer a simple prayer, "Jesus, I will deny myself and die daily in order to follow You. I will no longer live for myself."

If you just prayerfully read through these last few paragraphs, I celebrate with you over the greatest decision you will ever make in your life. You've just crossed over from death to life, from slavery to freedom, and from unforgiven to forgiven. You know you may not feel any different after making such an eternal decision, but remember, it's not about feelings, it's all about faith. Faith means that it's not about what you have done (or what you feel) but about trusting in what Christ has done for you.

CHAPTER 13

The Greatest Truth Ever Known

Some people have chosen a verse from the Bible as a "life verse." Let me encourage you to choose a verse that speaks to the greatest truth you've ever known or a verse that is the essence of who you are or who you desire to be. My life verse is 2 Corinthians 5:21, and it's at the core of what my life and this book is all about. In fact, it is perhaps the singular verse that has transformed my life more than any other. I want to share with you a hidden truth found in this verse that most people have never grasped.

> *"God made Him who had no sin to be sin for us, so that in Him we might become the righteousness of God."*
> *2 Corinthians 5:21*

The first half of this verse is what we've been exploring throughout this chapter. These twelve words, prior to the comma, explain the Gospel that most Christians have come to understand. God made Him (Jesus), who lived a sinless life, to become sin for us. He took our sin upon Himself and nailed it to the cross – killed it, destroyed it for us. The first half of this verse describes how we can *be* forgiven; the second half of this verse describes how we can *live* forgiven.

I know just enough Greek to be dangerous, and there is a key word here that unlocks the meaning of this verse. It's the word, *hina* in the Greek. It's the word following the comma that we've translated *so that*. The word *hina* in the Greek begins what is known as a "hina clause" in Greek syntax (the rules, patterns, or structure followed in the formation of Greek sentences). Hang with me. The hina clause is translated "in order that," and when you see it in a sentence it means that whatever was previously said was said "in order that" what is to follow might be said. In other words, one truth is presented so that another, and perhaps greater, truth might be understood. Such is the case here. Again, most people who hear the Gospel explained understand the first half of this verse; very few fully grasp the second half. And the second half of this verse is at the heart of what it means to *live forgiven*. If all I grasp here is the first half of this verse then the Gospel is simply "fire insurance," a ticket out of hell. Once I receive Christ, I'm done. I've crossed the finish line, because Christ died to take away my sin.

The first half of this verse explains what He's *taken from* me; the latter half of this verse explains what He's *given to* me. The first half tells me what I was; the second half tells me what I've become. He has taken away my sin; He's given me His righteousness. I was a sinner; I've now been made righteous.

What does it mean that you have become the "righteousness of God"? Don't miss this critical distinction: It is what you have become. It is who you are. If this is what I've "become" then what is it? If this is now who I am, then who am I? Oddly enough, or tragically enough, though this is at the very core of what it means to be a Christian, very few have embraced this truth.

To truly discover who we have become we must understand what the "righteousness of God is." How would you define the righteousness of God? I've asked this question many times, in private conversations and in larger groups. It's usually met with silence, which is tragic, because this is what we have become! I think the biggest problem among Christ's followers today is that we don't know who we are!

Simply put, the righteousness of God is His very character, His essence, His very nature. His righteousness is His justice, mercy, and grace wrapped up in one. His righteousness is, namely, His holiness. Even more tangibly perhaps, His righteousness is seen in the life of Jesus – to be righteous is to be *just like Jesus*. Think about this: You have become exactly like Jesus. I know what you're thinking, *Whoa, Jeff, there is no way! I am not exactly like Jesus*. Did you miss something? The Word of God says that you have "become the very righteousness of God in Him." Who do you want me to believe, you or God? Sorry, I'm going with God. Obviously I don't always live just like Jesus, so what does this mean?

I love the story of the father and his little son lying on the bed, reading a children's book together. The father told his son how much he loved him and the son said, "Love is when your daddy reads you a bedtime story, isn't it?" "That's right, son," said the sleepy father as he snuggled up with his son. "But true love," his son continued, "is when he doesn't skip any pages!"

Ah, yes, true love is when the father doesn't skip any pages. When it came to your forgiveness, God the Father didn't skip any pages. He has forgiven you completely. As we've noted, 2 Corinthians 5:21 tells us that He has not only taken away our sin but has replaced it with His righteousness. I love how the Living Bible puts it. This paraphrase of the Bible says it in a most powerful way and captures the essence of this verse. It says, "He poured our sin into Him and poured His righteousness into us." Imagine all of your sin being poured into Jesus and all that is Jesus – His goodness, His holiness, His righteousness – being poured into you!

Let me give you a fun scenario that will help you further grasp this reality. I've offered this illustration many times with groups of young people and adults to make the point. Imagine that I have invited a very special guest to join us today. *Here He is, ladies and gentlemen, Jesus Christ!* (I've actually motioned to the back of the room and have seen people turn their heads to see if He was actually coming in the room!) Of course, I would just bow down and let Him take the microphone.

I then pull up two chairs and ask someone from the audience to come sit in one of them. I'll ask the person if they have received Christ's forgiveness (having explained what He did for us on the cross). Imagine yourself in the chair as Jesus then sits in the chair beside *you*. If we were to ask the Father, *Who is more righteous, you or Jesus?* What would the Father say? How would you answer that question?

If you have received Christ as your Lord and Savior you have become the very "righteousness of God in Him." I know this sounds crazy, but you have become as righteous as Jesus is righteous. As God looks at you He sees you as fully forgiven, totally loved, and completely accepted, entirely approved by Him. Notice this happens because you are "in Him." This little phrase is loaded with significance and one that we will unpack throughout much of the rest of this book. What does it mean to be *in Him?* We'll explore this question in Section Four. How can we *stay* "in Him"? We'll look at this one in Section Five.

When I was in college I was an art major. And as a sophomore in college I knew everything there was to know about art. If you didn't think so, you could just ask me. One night my roommate and I were walking through a mall and came upon a watercolor exhibit. We stopped so I could peruse the paintings. My roommate followed along as I began to critique the artwork. "The composition in this one is way off," I suggested. "If the light source is coming from this direction, why are the shadows moving in this direction?" I asked, pointing out the flaws. I critiqued each painting as I continued to impress my roommate with my vast knowledge of art. (I was impressing myself at this point.)

After several minutes of this I suddenly heard a female voice behind me. "Oh, so you think you could do better?" As I turned around, I knew who spoke these words before I saw her. It was the artist! I was so embarrassed I don't even remember how I answered her. I'm sure it was something like, "Oh, no. These paintings are wonderful!" I was frozen, wanting to leave immediately.

But she was not done. She asked, "Do you see that sticker right there?" She pointed to a round sticker on the bottom right-hand corner of the painting. "Yes," I said sheepishly, "I see that sticker. I love that sticker. I like the color of that sticker and how you placed that sticker at just the right spot." (Okay, I didn't say all of that, but I wanted to.) I noticed the sticker was a price tag. She asked, "What does it say on that sticker?" I said, "Five hundred dollars." "That's right," she said. "Look at this one. What's this one say?" We looked at the price tag on the painting next to the previous one. "It's says seven hundred and fifty dollars," I said. She went on, "See that one over there? It will sell for fifteen hundred dollars. That one? Eight or nine hundred. I make my living selling these paintings. Obviously, some people think they're pretty good."

Wow. I learned a valuable lesson that day: Never talk about the artwork with the artist standing right behind you! Actually, I learned a much more powerful lesson that I've never forgotten. Crazy enough, it's a lesson that has helped me realize how much God loves me. The value of the painting is not determined by *my opinion* of the painting. The value of the painting is determined by what someone is *willing to pay* for the painting.

The value of your life is not determined by someone else's opinion of you. Neither is it determined by your own opinion of yourself. Your value, your significance, your price tag is determined by what God was willing to pay for your life.

James asks this question: "What is your life? You are a mist that appears for a little while and then vanishes" (James 4:14). We've been engaged in perhaps life's most important exercise: An assessment of how we are to live this one and only life that we've been given. A much-needed question in our culture today is how are we to value a single human life? Even in my lifetime, the value of the human life has diminished. This is reflected in our laws, the lack of love and respect toward individuals, and even in the absence of everyday kindness toward one another. We must get back to the value of every human life as God has placed a price tag on each of us. He alone is the One who places the priority, the value, the price, on every individual life.

Wired magazine ran an interesting article that asked the question, "What is the human body worth?"[18] They considered a purely physical value assessment of a person's body. Of course, their prices are hypothetical and drawn from hospitals and insurance companies. I'm pretty sure this breakdown is not only unethical and illegal, but impossible. The article noted that vital organs are no longer the most valuable body parts, rather it is bone marrow – priced at $23 million – based on 1,000 grams at $23,000 per gram. Your DNA is worth $9.7 million, while extracting antibodies could bring $7.3 million.

Then it listed a host of prices for vital organs with lungs topping the list ahead of kidneys and hearts. So in the end, you shouldn't feel like a million dollars anymore; you should feel more like $45 million! Now, before we start getting too cocky, this same article said that when the human body is broken down into its basic elements and minerals, it's actually worth about $4.50.

Of course, the point is that the Bible teaches us that our lives are much more than DNA, tissue, and organs. We all know that no one's body will last forever, but each body will ultimately die and decay. God's Word tells us that it is the souls of people that will live on forever, not our bodies – at least not as they are. Though man looks at the outward appearance, God looks at the heart. This is a seismic shift we must all make – only the souls of men and women have ultimate, eternal value. This is what God values the most. So now, from God's perspective, how much are you worth? God gave His One and Only Son for you. Jesus gave His life. He has placed an indescribable price tag on you.

1 Corinthians 6:20 says, "You were bought at a price. Therefore honor God with your body." You and I were bought with the highest price imaginable, the price of Christ's life for ours. God has already proclaimed the value of the human soul. He has already determined how much you are worth. It's not your opinion of yourself, it's not your performance, or the approval of others that determines your worth. It is the price of the precious blood of Jesus Christ that has determined your value forever. This is the great exchange. This is who you have become. This is who you are and nothing can change it. This is grace defined.

Questions to ponder:

1. How would you explain the central reason why Jesus came?

2. Again, in your own words, how would you define grace?

3. In the section on what really happened on the cross, what struck you the most?

4. How would you answer the question, "What is a Christian?"

5. Do you agree that the truth found in 2 Corinthians 5:21 just might be the greatest truth ever known? Why or why not?

Section Four
Defined By Grace

"The winds of grace are always blowing; all we need to do is raise our sails."
Anonymous

CHAPTER 14

What's Next is Now

Now that we've defined grace, let's consider how to be defined *by* grace. I've noted that every person must answer this question: Will I be defined by others, or will I define myself? Will I allow my life to be guided by how others define who I am, or will I determine to live my life according to how I define myself? I've also noted that the most well-adjusted people are not driven by the opinions of others. However, those who determine to define themselves have a problem that is not easily resolved. How do we overcome our *own* opinion of ourselves? How do we sort through our own misconceptions, presuppositions, and experiences in order to rightly define ourselves? These are the questions we'll address in this section. If you have determined to live forgiven let me challenge you; it's not a one-time decision but a daily determination to live a different kind of life. Your life is now on a new trajectory and it will take all you've got to stay on course.

A life defined by grace is the essence of what it means to be a Christian, and it's at the core of what Paul meant when he said, "Therefore, if anyone is in Christ, he is a new creation; the old has gone, the new has come!" (2 Corinthians 5:17). When you cross that line of faith you haven't finished the race; you've only just begun. In this chapter we'll explore some practical truths about who you have become in Christ. It all starts with what you *think*. You really can "be transformed by the renewing of your mind" (Romans 12:2).

As you learn to think differently you'll discover that you can *live* differently.

Once you receive the forgiveness of Jesus and decide to live in it, you resolve to accept no one's definition of your life. Not even your own. You no longer compare yourself to others because no one in the entire world can do a better job of being you than you. You learn to enjoy *being you*. We've recognized the importance of correctly defining oneself. The greater truth is that we must define ourselves not by what *we* think or what anybody else thinks, but by what *God* thinks. Primarily because He's always right and we seldom are. What He thinks is evidenced by what He's already said about us and by what He's already done for us on the cross. It's a tricky proposition to think God's thoughts and not our own thoughts because we *do* think, don't we? "I think, therefore I am," was essentially Rene Descartes' entire ontology.[19] Our thinking really does define our existence.

Socrates noted, "The only true wisdom is in knowing you know nothing." Five hundred years earlier, Paul had already said it better: "The man who thinks he knows something does not yet know as he ought to know" (1 Corinthians 8:2). The problem is, of course, we *do* know something, and when it comes to what we *know* about ourselves, most of it is wrong. If you've lived long at all you know a lot, and much of what you know may not be the truth.

The discipline of reprogramming the mind might just be the greatest of all disciplines and the beginning of every other. You and I have our own unique experience of life and a set of "recordings" that we play out in our minds every day. It's been said that we count our lives in years, but we remember our lives in moments. If you took some time and worked hard enough you could think of moments that have defined much of who you are. Some of these moments are vivid; some are fuzzy. Some are public; some are very private. Some remain in secret, only in your memory. How you've interpreted some of these moments is how the lies about yourself were born. In the introduction I presented the five greatest deterrents to a proper understanding of God and a life of grace. Consider them again:

1. A lack of exposure to biblical grace
2. Graceless Christians and graceless preaching and teaching
3. Unloving or graceless parents (namely, fathers)
4. A misunderstanding of evil and suffering
5. An unwillingness to appropriate the grace of God in relationships

Of the five, which ones have you experienced in your life? Any one of these negative influences can warp a proper view of self. Unless we reprogram our thinking, these deterrents plant lies within us that become a regular part of our thinking. You did not become who you are overnight nor did you develop a pattern of thinking in a day or two. Your journey to a grace-filled life is a journey, and for most of us it's a long one. Perhaps you've come to think that you will never overcome some of these deep-rooted thoughts about who you are. You've determined you'll never change. If so, I would suggest that's yet another lie you've come to believe. You *can* change, and you're already on the verge of the greatest change you've ever experienced.

If you're like me you're tempted to fall into the trap of waiting for whatever is coming next. Too many times in my life I've missed the present while looking for what's coming. I've always been wired to look ahead, explore what is just around the corner. As a leader I tend to live in the future, probably to a fault. Do you ever do this? Are you always looking for the next thing to come along? I suppose that's a good thing most of the time, but when it comes to a life forgiven it's good to look at what's *already* happened – what's *already* been completed. Many Christians believe all the good stuff that God has planned for us is in heaven, and they live their lives as if the good stuff is found *only* in heaven. I am convinced that heaven is a real place and I can't wait to experience it, but God wants me to experience the good stuff now!

As stated earlier, the biggest difference between religion and Christianity is that religion is spelled "do" while Christianity is spelled "done." For the person who has embraced the grace of Christ, it's important to realize that what comes next is already here. It's what theologians call "realized eschatology." It is eschatology (pertaining to end times and the completion of God's redemptive work in the world) that is realized because what is to come has already been set in motion. It's already done.

On one occasion the Pharisees asked Jesus when the kingdom of God would come (as if they didn't already have an immoveable opinion), and Jesus explained, "The kingdom of God does not come with careful observation, nor will people say, 'Here it is,' or 'There it is,' because the kingdom of God is within you" (Luke 17:21). There is a mysterious quality to the kingdom. It's come, it's here, and it's coming. Jesus taught us to pray for God's will to be done and His kingdom to come "on earth as it is in heaven" (Matthew 6:10). This is a profound truth: What's next is now.

One of the great truths of salvation is that it is at once – past, present, and future. Once you decide to live as a kingdom person you enter into a kind of *Twilight Zone* where the past, present, and future all come together. You see, on the cross Jesus set in motion the potential for His redemptive love to transform my life. You could say that it was then that I *was* saved. His redemptive work was not appropriated in my life until I was personally saved when I received His grace as my own. I *was* saved and I *am* saved right now because of His ongoing redemptive work in my life. I *will be* saved when my salvation is fully realized as I enter heaven to live on in perfect union and worship of Him. But again, we don't need to wait because our eschatology (what's next...) is realized (now). This is a major shift for a lot of Christians – to realize that the Kingdom is not some far-off place. It *is* coming, but it's happening right now!

Of the many metaphors of life perhaps the one I relate to the most is that of a race. I suppose in part that's why I'm a triathlete. Or perhaps it's the other way around; I'm a triathlete because of what it teaches me about life. Apart from its therapeutic effects on me, I love the challenge of finishing a race, persevering on to the finish line. Some of my life's greatest lessons have come through the sport. Perhaps you are or have been an athlete – a walker or a cyclist – and you can relate. The amazing thing about life *in Christ* is that as we run this race of life we do so knowing that the race has already been finished. In Philippians 3:12, Paul spoke of running this race and described it this way: "Not that I have already obtained all this" (that is, a sinless life with Christ) "or have already been made perfect, but I press on to take hold of that for which Christ Jesus took hold of me."

We live in this tension of "already" and "not yet." I'm certain, however, that most of us live in the "not yet" much more than we live in the "already." Notice that Christ "took hold" of Paul so that he might experience all that Christ had already taken hold of for him; namely, a life forgiven. The "already" gives us hope while we persevere in the "not yet." Jesus is helping us complete a race that He's already finished. This is why you can live a confident life. "…He who began a good work in you will carry it on to completion until the Day of Christ Jesus" (Philippians 1:6). As you partner with Jesus to be defined by grace and live forgiven He will not let you go. In this section I want you to learn how to settle into this "already" but "not yet" tension that is the forgiven life. It all begins when you realize that what's next is now.

CHAPTER 15

You *Are* Who You Think You Are

It's been said that low self-esteem is like going through life with the handbrake on. What I'm talking about here is much more than self-esteem, self-fulfillment, or self-talk, but perhaps you have allowed negative and harmful recordings to play over and over in your mind. Maybe you don't really know what it is to live without the constant friction of a life hindered by the handbrake of a misguided image of yourself. It's time to release the brake. You now sit atop a giant hill and it's time to go for it. Freedom awaits, and you will experience it as you determine to be defined by grace and not by the recordings you've listened to for so long. I want to help you erase your play list and start over with some songs you desperately need to hear. In fact, let's tag them under favorites and allow them to be the most played music in your life. God wants you to live in the constant music of His amazing grace – how sweet the sound.

Proverbs 23:7 says, "As a man thinks, so is he," and you have now entered into a new way of thinking. What *recordings* have you allowed to define who you are? In order to experience this newfound freedom you must decide that you will no longer be defined by the recordings that have played in your mind for so long. What negative words or experiences define your life to this point? You can no longer allow these experiences, failures, or the approval of others to define you. If you have received Christ you truly are a new creation, with new thoughts, a new mission, and a new future.

Hope for a brighter future drives us forward, and surely there is coming a day when we will no longer struggle with the weight of sin. But again way too many Christians seem to simply be waiting on heaven. Vance Havner once said, "Some Christians have become so heavenly minded that they are of no earthly good." We're waiting to change in "the sweet by and by" (whatever that means), and we need to realize that we don't have to wait for heaven to experience the joy of living in His grace. Shall we trample on the precious sacrifice of Jesus by not fighting to appropriate this costly grace into our lives every day?

You must take on the *mind of Christ*. In fact, 1 Corinthians 2:16 says, "…we *have* the mind of Christ." Followers of Jesus are to think differently about our God, ourselves, and our world. To be continually defeated by the same wrong thoughts about ourselves over and over again is sin. The writer of Hebrews offers some strong language about this kind of habitual sin. In Hebrews 10:29 he asks, "How much more severely do you think a man deserves to be punished who has trampled the Son of God underfoot, who has treated as an unholy thing the blood of the covenant that sanctified him, and who has insulted the Spirit of grace?" Whoa, this reprogramming of the mind is serious stuff. Though the forgiveness of Jesus has already taken place, our ability, our willingness to live in it is a daily battle. It all starts as you reprogram your thinking.

As we think about taking on the *mind of Christ*, let's consider what *was* going on in the mind of Christ. People may wonder *What would Jesus do?* but consider, *"What would Jesus think?* He never once thought, *Man, I'm such a loser* or *I'll never overcome my past* or *Wow, I wish I could be like that guy*. Jesus lived the perfect life, because His actions were born out of perfect thoughts. Divine thoughts led to a divine life.

You *are* who you think you are. And who you are has already been determined. You don't have to wait on it. When Jesus "became flesh and made His dwelling among us" (John 1:14) He offered to us "the exact representation of God's character" (Hebrews 1:3). You could say that when God spoke "Jesus" nothing more needed to be said. And when Jesus spoke *His* final words, He offered a summary of His entire life on earth.

In chapter 12 we examined the death of Jesus in great detail. We explored the power behind His words indicating that the Father had abandoned Him. As He hung on that cross He uttered three other words – His very last three words – that culminated His life's purpose. Before He breathed His final breath, He said, "It is finished" (John 19:30). In the Greek, it's one word: *tetelestai.* Luke 23:46 tells us that He said His final words "with a loud voice;" Mark 15:37 says, "with a loud cry."

These words were not a declaration of defeat. These were not words of surrender. They were the triumphant cry of a warrior who had won the battle, a runner who had finished the race. Jesus had finished the race, but He did not simply mean that His earthly life was over. He meant that the work the Father sent Him to do was now complete. He had finished His goal, accomplished His task; He had fulfilled His purpose. And He meant that He had crossed the finish line for us – *our* finish line. But what did He "finish" for us? What is it that He already "took hold of" (Philippians 3:12), and how can I connect the past (what Christ has done) to the present (what I'm doing in my life today)? How can I transform my thinking around what has already happened – and will *never* change? When He said, "It is finished," He meant that:

• **He finished the perfect life.**

If you struggle to accept yourself because of your past and present mistakes, here's a news flash: You don't have to be perfect. As noted, God's holiness demanded a perfect sacrifice, one without blemish. Jesus was, "… tempted in every way just as we are, yet was without sin" (Hebrews 4:15). By living the perfect life Christ did for us what we could not do for ourselves. He alone could die on the cross because He alone lived the perfect life. Without the perfect life the sacrifice would not have been complete.

Think about how this should change your thinking. You don't have to be perfect in order to feel good about yourself, because Christ has finished the perfect life for you. When God the Father looks at you He sees the perfect life of Jesus covering you. I do press on, however, to strive toward excellence. Not because I'm obligated to do so or so that God will like me more. I do so because of my love for Jesus and because I want to live just like Him. My motivation for change is driven by my gratitude for all He has done and is for me.

- **He finished the payment for our sin.**

Because your sin is forgiven, you are already made perfect in the eyes of God. Though "all have sinned and fall short of the glory of God" (Romans 3:23), your sin has been completely paid for by Christ. While our sin has consequences, He paid a debt that we owed but couldn't pay. The price for our sin was paid through Christ's sacrifice upon the cross.

- **He finished the punishment for our sin.**

You no longer need to punish yourself for your sin. Though I constantly need to confess my sin and turn from it, Christ has taken all the punishment upon Himself. God's holy wrath was satisfied on the cross. Because Jesus took it upon Himself I no longer have to think condemning thoughts about myself. The sacrificial Lamb of God finished the need for my life to be a sacrifice to make things right between me and God. I no longer have to live in that tension.

- **He finished the need for religion.**

No longer do you need to seek God's approval through some religious activity. You no longer have to be good enough. You can live at ease with God, not in the constant "dis-ease" of trying to be good enough. You can now experience a religion-free life of peace. When Jesus said, "It is finished" He removed the need for religion.

- **He finished the pathway to eternal life.**

This is big. You can now live with an eternal mindset that impacts how you think about everything. Because your future has been determined you can live with a constant hope and an optimism that drives every day of your life. The hope that you have for eternal life is made certain through Jesus Christ because He finished the race that you could not run. When He said, "I am the Way and the Truth and the Life. No one comes to the Father except through me" (John 14:6). He was announcing a Way that had already been established that would never change. Notice the present tense of Christ's promise: He *is* the Way. The hope that you now have is in a future that has been made secure. You think differently about the future because it is certain.

The fact that Jesus finished the race for you means that you have a decision to make. You must determine that you will fully embrace what He has accomplished for you. God's great dream for you to live forgiven must become your own. You must choose to be defined by the grace of God. If you and I can learn the rhythm of grace and decide that a life forgiven will be our singular pursuit then we can experience what Eugene Peterson has called, *A Long Obedience in the Same Direction*.[20] This is the race that we were created to run with God. If we remain faithful we will be able to join Paul who near the end of his life said, "I have fought the good fight, I have finished the race, I have kept the faith" (2 Timothy 4:7). A new day has come and a new adventure awaits you. Are you ready? The start and finish lines are one and the same. You're already a winner because what's next is now and you *are* who you think you are.

CHAPTER 16

Your Identity Has Been Redefined

One day two caterpillars were crawling along and a beautiful butterfly flew by. They saw its massive wings as it fluttered by and one caterpillar said to the other, "You'll never get me up in one of those things." Most of us cannot imagine what we've been created to become. And fewer still ever realize their fullest potential. You and I have been created by God to soar beautifully in this life, with incredible potential for love, sacrifice, and great joy. But most of us spend our days lumbering along on the ground of unrealized potential that is waiting to be born in us. Every now and then you meet someone who's truly gone through that miraculous transformation of the heart and you think, *I want to live like that.* But like the caterpillar, if you don't go through a process of radical transformation, you'll just remain a caterpillar.

I'm convinced that the reason people don't reach their full potential is because they never fully embrace their new identity found in Christ. We noted from the outset that *you're not who you think you are,* and once you come to Christ you realize you're not who you were. You have a brand-new identity out of which this entire new life flows. Your first step is to replace your old identity with the new. For everything you once felt or believed about yourself, God has a new way of thinking and living each day.

The following illustrates why the Gospel, this Good News of what Christ has done for you, is so relevant in your life today. With each new reality presented below there is a corresponding theological truth that defines your new position in Christ. As you realize how your identity has been redefined, you'll see why His forgiveness is the gateway to a life of freedom. Once forgiven, there are five seismic shifts that have taken place. You're no longer who you used to be.

• **From condemnation to commendation**

Here's a big one for many: Once you embrace the unfathomable grace of God made available to you, you must determine that self-condemnation will end. You are now totally accepted by God, and the moment that you choose not to live in that acceptance you are choosing not to embrace the forgiven life. In essence, you are denying the truth of His grace made alive in you.

In one of the most powerful stories of grace found in the Bible, Jesus is faced with a defining moment in His ministry when a group of Pharisees bring a woman caught in adultery to Him. Even if you haven't read much of the Bible, you may have heard this story. Jesus stands between the accused woman and the religious leaders and says, "If any one of you is without sin, let Him be the first to throw a stone at her" (John 8:7). The woman, crouched over, anticipating the sound and impact of the first stone, hears instead the sound of stones dropping to the ground. Ultimately each man leaves. The next thing she hears is Jesus. "Woman, where are they? Has no one condemned you?" "No one, sir," she said. "Then neither do I condemn you," Jesus declared. "Go now and leave your life of sin" (John 8:10-11).

When you beat yourself up in a moment (or perhaps throughout a lifetime) of self-condemnation you are rejecting the costly, horrific condemnation of Jesus. He has been condemned so that your condemnation would end. This is why Romans 8:1 says, "Therefore, there is now no condemnation for those who are in Christ Jesus." When you condemn yourself you are dismissing and discrediting the sufficient work of Jesus on the cross.

1 John 1:9-10 gives us God's solution to our condemnation. It says that Jesus has become the *propitiation* for our sin. This word means *satisfaction* or *atonement*. Notice the interesting breakdown of that word, *at-one-ment*. It means that we are now *at one* with

God because Christ became "God's atoning sacrifice." He became God's *wrath satisfier*. We saw earlier that wrath is simply God's holy reaction to sin. Jesus took on the divine wrath of God so you wouldn't have to. He took on your punishment so you don't have to be punished. And you don't have to blame others or continue to hold their sin over them. You no longer have to punish others.

God's answer to my condemnation is actually commendation. He now approves of me, and instead of condemning me He actually supports me. He blesses me. Jesus even intercedes for me. He becomes my Advocate. Romans 8:34 says, "Who is He that condemns? Christ Jesus, who died – more than that, who was raised to life – is at the right hand of God and is also interceding for us." If anyone is in position to condemn or "throw the first stone" it is Jesus, and yet He does not condemn us. He intercedes (intervenes, pleads on our behalf, acts as the mediator) for us! You can stop condemning yourself and others. You have a new identity; now live in it. Christ was condemned so that you would never be again.

- **From blame to acclaim**

   As we noted in Chapter 2, blame says *I have done something wrong and I deserve to be punished*. I think too often we confuse the consequences of our sin with the punishment of God. We end up blaming God for our own decisions. No doubt you and I pay the consequences of our sin because that's precisely the way God set it up. We learn best through natural consequences; at least that's the way it's supposed to be.

   I'm not talking about the consequences of sin. I'm talking about a constant blaming of self and others for wrong done. Are you quick to look for blame when something goes wrong? Do you constantly blame yourself or others? God's answer to this life of blaming is called *justification*. Romans 4:25 says, "Christ was delivered over for our sins and was raised to life for our justification." This word justification was a word from the world of law which means, "a judicial vindication" or "acquittal." It is a verdict of *not guilty*. When one is justified she or he is *made right*, pronounced *not guilty*. I've been exonerated. I am no longer guilty before a holy God. I am fully approved by Him and no longer live a life of blame. I am actually *acclaimed* by God as His son or daughter. With my new identity I no longer want to blame myself and others. I can stop punishing others for wrongs done to me. I can seek to forgive and mend broken relationships. I can release myself from the punishment I think I deserve. I can also set others free from the punishment I think they may deserve.

- **From humiliation to reconciliation**

Humiliation is shame. Psychiatrists tell us that if blame says, "I have done wrong," then shame says, "I *am* wrong." I know many people who live with a deep sense of shame. It's as if they are constantly thinking, *I am always wrong, I will always be wrong, I cannot change.* The devastating and debilitating thing about shame is that it moves a step beyond blame. Shame says, *I cannot change and do not deserve to move beyond my punishment.* Like many therapists and counselors, I've seen self-inflicted cuts and wounds on people who have lived with a deep sense of shame. It's interesting to note that there is within each of us a deep sense that someone must pay for our shame.

A side note here: I think that Satan's easiest door to shame is through sexual sin. I have seen more shame-filled people as a result of sexual sin or abuse than any other type of sin. And like fungus and mushrooms, shame grows in the dark. This is why we must expose our past experiences in the light. It's why the Bible says, "Therefore confess your sins to each other and pray for each other so that you may be healed. The prayer of a righteous man is powerful and effective" (James 5:16). We really are only as sick as our secrets. Self-mutilation comes in many forms – cutting, abusing the body, over-medicating, over-drinking, *over*-anything. It comes from a person who thinks, they must pay for their sin. My "wrongness" must be paid for and I'm the one who must pay. As noted, you will *never* be able to pay for your sin.

God's answer to shame is another fancy Bible word: reconciliation. Romans 5:10 says, "…we were enemies of God but now are *reconciled* through the death of His Son…" You have been brought back into a right relationship with God. You were once guilty of sin and needed to pay the price for it. Now you are totally accepted by God and completely loved by Him. Living in your new identity means that you no longer have to pay the price for your sin (or force others to pay the price). It also means that you *can* change and you *can* relate to others in such a way that says, *I believe you can change too. I am not who I am becoming and neither are you.* I don't have to hold others' sins over them. I can release them and stop *punishing* them for wrongs done to me. My new identity in Christ means that I am free from shame.

- **From abandoned to adopted**

Among other places, Hebrews 13:5 says, "I will never leave you, nor forsake you." If you have ever felt that God has left you alone, be certain He did not. Christ was abandoned so that you would *never* be abandoned by God. The Bible says that Jesus became "derelict." This literally means that He became like "a ship abandoned at sea, a person or place abandoned by its owner or occupant." It implies an "intentional or conscious neglect, forgotten." Or to use the language of our day: He became "road kill" for us. Not only dying but left alone dying. Again it seems that we have underestimated the sacrifice of Jesus and what He has taken *away* from us. So remember, even if you feel alone, you are not. Once you were like Him, like a ship abandoned at sea, but now you have a new identity in Him. Christ was forsaken so that you and I would never be abandoned.

In fact, like everything else He does, God went "over the top" to make sure that you would never feel abandoned again. His answer to this sense of being left alone – derelict, abandoned – that we are prone to feel is *adoption*. He has given us a new family by adopting us into His!

Recently my brother, Kevin, and his wife, Beth, adopted a little boy named Taylor.[21] During the process I realized anew the precious act of grace that is adoption. I discovered that an adoptive family looks a lot more like the family of God than one biologically formed. Taylor is now a member of a family into which he was not born. He's in a family that he knew nothing about. His father and mother went all the way to Russia to get him. They traveled thousands of miles to get him and bring him back to be in their family. Taylor now has a new home. In Christ, God came to fetch us. He came down – from the *very top* He came down – to bring us back home with Him.

Consider these verses in Ephesians 1:4-6: "For He chose us in Him before the creation of the world to be holy and blameless in His sight. In love He predestined us to be adopted as His sons through Jesus Christ, in accordance with His pleasure and will – to the praise of His glorious grace, which He has freely given us in the One He loves." Don't miss this. Adoption indicates choice ahead of obligation. God was not obligated to love you; He chose to love you. He chooses *you*! He planned ahead of time that you would be made *holy* – without blame and without shame. Because of His "glorious grace" you have been totally accepted, fully loved, and adopted into His family as a son or daughter.

Jesus stood trial so that you might have an Advocate. He was wounded so that you would be healed. He was condemned so that you could be set free. He was forsaken by the Father so that you would never be rejected. The Father abandoned the Son so that you would never be abandoned. Never! Not today, not in your deepest, darkest moments of pain and abandonment. And... not in that moment when you too will face death and be ushered into the presence of the One who has promised, "I will never leave you, nor forsake you." And as you move into eternity, at your final breath, He is there to usher you into a life that you can begin to live today. Too many Christians live as if *some day* they'll really experience life as it was meant to be. Jesus would say that you and I need to determine to be defined by grace because what's next is *now*.

Like the caterpillar that could not imagine itself a butterfly, perhaps you need to embrace this transformation that has happened (and *is* happening) in your life. It's time to spread your wings and fly by living in this new identity. It will take everything you've got, and your love for Christ compels you to do it. You need to discipline your mind to think new thoughts that reflect the new truth that you have discovered. In Christ you are no longer a fuzzy caterpillar but a beautiful butterfly. You've become a new creation transformed by God from the inside out.

In Romans 12:2 Paul put it this way: "Do not conform any longer to the pattern of this world, but be transformed by the renewing of your mind. Then you will be able to test and approve what God's will is – His good, pleasing and perfect will." One of the primary ways you can transform your mind is through Scripture. You need to rid yourself of former thoughts and replace them with the truth of God's Word.

Most Christians think of a pure and disciplined mind in terms of what we are *not* to think about. As I noted earlier we tend to go toward the negative – what we're *against* instead of what we're *for* – what we don't want to think about instead of what we should be thinking about. Maybe that's not a "Christian" thing but a human thing. We tend to move toward the negative. But that's only half the equation. You can't stop thinking certain thoughts unless you replace them with new thoughts.

Let me walk you through a mental exercise to make my point. Imagine the number four. Put the image of this number four clearly in your mind. Now, forget about the number four. Just stop imagining this number four that you've put in your mind. Go ahead, stop thinking about the number four. You can't. Of course, it doesn't help for me to continue to remind you of it.

Now take the number four and multiply it by two. Add four to that number and then subtract six. Are you with me? Now add three. What do have now? You should have nine (unless you're doing some of that "new math" we talked about earlier). I just "renewed" your mind; or should I say, you did. You replaced your focus on the number four (yikes, there it is again!) with the number nine. Notice you did this not by simply trying to rid yourself of the number four but by replacing it through a process. Your mind was "transformed, by the renewing of your mind." This is how the Word of God works. If you are to live in this new identity you must replace old thoughts with new ones. You will develop the "mind of Christ" as you remove and replace.

As you consider the thoughts that you're prone to have, perhaps you've realized a need to renew your mind with the truth of God about you. What lies are you prone to think? What are some recurring insecurities or tendencies you have? Below I've offered the truth about your new identity and a corresponding verse that will help you in the transformation process. Pick the truth that you need to be reminded of the most and memorize the verse. As you face moments in which you are tempted to retreat to your old way of thinking, you'll be armed to combat them with a new way of thinking.

My New Identity in Christ[22]

- **I am completely loved by God.**
  "This is love: not that we loved God, but that He loved us and sent His Son as an atoning sacrifice for our sins." 1 John 4:10

- **I am entirely forgiven by God.**
  "Therefore, there is now no condemnation for those who are in Christ Jesus." Romans 8:1

- **I am fully pleasing to God.**
  "Therefore, since we have been justified through faith, we have peace with God through our Lord Jesus Christ." Romans 5:1

- **I am totally accepted by God.**
  "But now He has reconciled you by Christ's physical body through death to present you holy in His sight, without blemish and free from accusation." Colossians 1:22

- **I am absolutely committed to God.**
  "I have been crucified with Christ and I no longer live, but Christ lives in me. The life I live in the body, I live by faith in the Son of God, who loved me and gave Himself for me." Galatians 2:20

These truths express the reality of your new identity in Christ. Make no mistake about it, you are a new creation. Therefore, you can live absolutely committed to Him. And remember, you are not alone. We can "…approach the throne of grace with confidence, so that we may receive mercy and find grace to help us in our time of need" (Hebrews 4:16). Notice that it says we can "find grace." We can live in this grace as we seek after this grace from the One who has promised to walk this journey with us! And again, what is our motivation? "For Christ's love compels us, because we are convinced that one died for all, and therefore all died" (2 Corinthians 5:14). It is the love of Christ that compels us, guides us, and sustains us. It all starts and ends with this love of our great God. Your identity has been redefined. What the caterpillar calls the end, the butterfly calls the beginning.

CHAPTER 17

Your Past Has Been Rewritten

This week I talked to a friend who cannot shake his past. In fact, though he realizes it's illogical, he can't shake the thought that others he loves are now being punished because of sins *he* committed in the past. Often it's not God punishing us over past sin, it's ourselves. Though we've been totally forgiven, we can't forgive ourselves.

I read the story of a guy who came down with amnesia and could not remember a thing about his wife of twenty years. The story told of the couple's newfound love for each other as they are now forced to start over. As I read this touching story I thought maybe amnesia is not all bad. Really, wouldn't it be great if you could simply forget some things you've done in the past? (I'm reminded of soldiers after the end of WWII, continuing to fight because they didn't know the war was over). If the war is already over then there's no need to fight anymore. Is it possible to live with a kind of "spiritual amnesia"? Can I stop fighting now that I realize the war is over?

In Philippians 3:13, Paul says, "Brothers, I do not consider myself yet to have taken hold of it. But one thing I do: Forgetting what lies behind and straining toward what is ahead..." Notice that Paul says, "one thing" and then he mentions *two things*. He says that he forgets what is behind and he strains toward what is ahead. He's simply saying that you can't do one without the other. They are one and the same. You will never move forward in this new life if you do not leave behind the stuff of your past. Is it possible to actually forget? Can I make myself forget? And if I could, would I cease to be me? Isn't memory a critical characteristic of who I am?

In his work, *The Eternal Now*, Paul Tillich noted, "The simple word 'forget' can plunge us into the deepest riddles of life and death, of time and eternity. The Bible abounds in its use. For forgetting and remembering are two of the most astonishing qualities by which the divine image in man is made manifest."[23] I don't know about you, but I can't *choose* to forget anything. But could it be that I become so determined to live in my new identity that it's *as if* I have forgotten who I used to be? I think this is entirely possible but only through the power of Christ as I partner with Him (more on that later).

The first step to "forgetting what lies behind and straining toward what is ahead" is to leave some things behind. Again, the butterfly offers a fitting analogy of what this process should look like. The transformation of a caterpillar to a butterfly serves as nature's equivalence of God's transformation in us. Why didn't God create the butterfly in the same way He created other creatures of flight? Why doesn't it just pop out of an egg and start flying around? Why this crazy transformation from one living thing that crawls laboriously on the ground to one that migrates thousands of miles across the earth?

Let's go back to third grade and the observation of the butterfly. You're probably aware that the butterfly actually starts out as a caterpillar, but the caterpillar starts out as an egg. Once a suitable site is found, the egg-laying, or oviposition, can take place. The female butterfly finds the perfect spot and the egg is laid. From the egg comes not a butterfly but a caterpillar, or larva. During the larva stage it eats so much that it grows up to one hundred times its original size. After the larva stage it moves on to the pre-pupa stage in which it crawls around looking for a good place to pupate. That's when it attaches itself to a plant and an amazing transformation takes place. During this stage it forms a pupa or chrysalis. The word chrysalis is derived from a Greek word meaning "gold," referring to the color of some Nymphalid pupae. The word "pupa" is the scientific word describing this stage of a butterfly's life.

Hang with me. Here's where it gets interesting. A hormone is introduced into its system, and it begins the process of becoming a new insect altogether. The chrysalis (or pupa) hangs down from a branch or ledge and in as little as two weeks a butterfly appears. After it transforms into a butterfly, the cocoon becomes transparent and you can actually see the butterfly inside. As it fights to break free from the cocoon, this struggle sends the proper transforming fluid throughout the butterfly's body. If the struggle is not great enough then the process is stopped, and it will never become a butterfly. Isn't that amazing? I would suggest only God can do that.

I share all of that not simply because it's so cool but because it is an apt comparison to our lives in Christ. We are caterpillars. We're really not much to look at. We're kind of slow on our feet and not getting anywhere fast. Food for birds is what we are. But then Jesus clothes us "in Him" and starts His transforming work. Yes, there's always a struggle of faith, but without the struggle, we'll never fly. If a butterfly could, do you think it would ever want to go back to being a caterpillar? No way! The gift of flight opens up a whole new world to explore and enjoy! God has done the same for us. He has made us a new creation; the old has gone and a new adventure has just begun!

Given the choice, I can't imagine the caterpillar would ever want to go back to who he was. *If* the butterfly *could* remember, certainly he would never go back. In fact, it seems to me that the more the butterfly could remember what it's like to be a caterpillar the more pleasure he would find in being who he is. I think that's what God desires in us. Perhaps that's why God has given us our spiritual memories. I'm reminded of the Israelites, who were set free from slavery in Egypt, but still wanted to return. In our newfound freedom, surely we would never want to go back to a life of slavery. Or would we?

I don't think most of us have truly grasped how deep this change is that God has birthed within us. To be defined by grace is not just a mind game. Like all things spiritual there's a greater reality beneath the surface. We don't just think our way into a new reality; there actually *is* a new reality and we can live in it. We have been changed at the very core of who we are. It's a change from the inside out.

You could say we have been infused with a whole new spiritual DNA. Here's perhaps the most amazing thing about the metamorphosis of the butterfly: The caterpillar and the butterfly are actually completely different at the molecular level. Did you know that the chemistry of the caterpillar and the butterfly are different? During that pupa stage, while in the cocoon, something truly miraculous takes place. In the end, a brand-new insect emerges.

This is exactly what happens when you come to Christ and allow Him to do His redemptive work in you. You become a new "creature" – a brand-new creation. I suppose we could argue that the butterfly can't remember a thing about being a caterpillar because it wasn't him! In a real sense, we do the same. The Bible says that when you receive Christ's forgiveness you have passed from death to life, from the flesh to the spirit, from sin to forgiveness, from darkness into light, and from the temporal to the eternal. You are truly a new creature. You have a new Father. You're in a new family, and you have new brothers and sisters. You have a new mind and you have a new Master. But most of us don't live that way, do we? Perhaps it's in part because this analogy does break down, doesn't it? I'm still me, it seems. You are still you.

Even if I could forget, what would I forget and what would I choose to remember? Alas, I cannot do either. I *do* remember and who I *was* seems to be hanging around a lot these days. It seems the answer to this dilemma lies in two possibilities: I either live *as if* I can't remember, or I live in complete memory of who I was. The former seems rather ingenuous or inauthentic – as if I'm trying to escape the reality of my past. The latter seems more painful and confusing – as if I'm living two different lives in two different worlds. Or am I? What if I remember in order to more fully embrace and rejoice in this new person I've become? I think that's exactly what it means to be saved now *and* not yet. Maybe remembering who I was is integral to living forgiven. Maybe I remember but live forgiven.

And if you think I'm chasing a rabbit, I can assure you I am not. This is huge. How do you live? Have you sought to pretend as if certain things have never happened in your life? Have you tried to brush some of your deepest secrets under the proverbial rug? If so, has it worked? Your past continues to rise up, doesn't it? I talk to people all the time who can't seem to shake a particular sin of their past. I've been in deeply moving spiritual moments with others as they've confessed sin, and I'm often shocked at how long ago these things happened. How tragic! Christ didn't die on the cross so that we would continue to be plagued by the sins of our past. He suffered and died so that we would be completely free! So all of this begs the question: How do I live in this tension of "forgetting what lies behind" and "pressing on toward what is ahead" when I can't seem to forget the very worst about me? Let's consider how to apply this aspect of God's grace so that we can live, once and for all, forgiven.

Could it be that the answer doesn't lie in us, but in God? (Hey, a recurring theme is developing here.) Could it be that God can do something we can't do? Namely, forget. Now, I can tell this is going to take us into the same place where we'll find questions like *Which came first the chicken or the egg?* or *Can God create a rock so big He can't move it?* or *Was Sanjaya the greatest American Idol contestant of all time?* Can God actually cause Himself to forget something? And if so, could He then cause Himself to remember it again? (I know, I couldn't help myself.)

Isaiah 43:25 says, ""I, even I, am He who blots out your trans-gressions, for my own sake, and remembers your sins no more." Jeremiah 31:34 says, "... I will forgive their wickedness and will remember their sins no more." This verse is quoted again in Hebrews 8:12. The Bible says that God chooses to forget my sins. Psalm 103:12 says, "As far as the east is from the west, so far has He removed our transgressions from us." Isaiah 38:17 says, "You have put all my sins behind your back." God has put all of my sins out of sight; He no longer *sees* me in light of my sins.

I think what God is trying to tell us is this: If He chooses to forget my sins then why do I hold on to them? And if He chooses not to remember my sin, then what does He do when I keep bringing them to Him again and again? I've wondered at times during a heart felt moment of confession if God doesn't just go, *Huh?* (I realize God probably never goes *huh?*, but if He did He would do it a lot with me.) I wonder if He ever hears us and thinks *What are you talking about? I've already "forgotten" that.* God's clever that way, you know. He can remember what He forgot… huh?

Think about it. If you can't remember something can you really forgive someone of it? It seems the greater act of grace is to remember fully, perhaps in great detail, a particular wrong and yet totally forgive the offender. I think that's really the way it is. God can do whatever He wants, but I think that He's wanting you and me to know that our sins are forgiven and it's *as if* they never happened. Think about your life *as if* certain things that you're most ashamed of never happened. What if all your mistakes, all your failures, and that *one* worst sin of your life never happened? Would your life be different? Would you think differently about yourself? I think you would more than you know. That's precisely the way God sees you. He sees you and relates to you as if those things never happened. He is not at all concerned about your past. He is, however, very interested in your future.

Your life is a story, and God is in the process of rewriting it. Of course, you know that your life is a story because that's how you experience it every day. Life is not a math problem; it comes to us as a story. There are all kinds of characters, scenes, and plots. Each day is like a paragraph, every month a page, and a year goes by like a chapter from a novel. Madeleine L'Engle noted, "All of life is a story." The problem is this: Most of us don't realize that life really is a story. And every story has an Author. Most of us live our lives as if we've opened a novel somewhere in the middle and we're trying to figure out what's going on. We know there's a grander story. Something big, something wonderful, even beautiful is happening, but we can't figure out the plot.

The problem is this: we've lost our story. Or I should say we've lost *God's* Story. When Solomon said, "God has planted eternity in the human heart" (Ecclesiastes 3:11), he meant that we all have an intuitive sense of the greater Story. Most of us have forgotten that the story we find ourselves in is the Story of God. His story (history) has been going on for a long time. Of course, the key to life is finding your place in the grand Story of God because you do have a role, a part to play. Paul Harvey reminds us that we really need to know the "rest of the story" if it's to make any sense. Here's the point: When you join the Story of God (by receiving His grace) you allow Him to rewrite your past and then, day by day, you allow Him to pen your future.

Because my story has been rewritten...

- **I can choose to rewrite my past in light of God's grace.**

Rewriting my past doesn't mean I can erase the consequences of my decisions of the past. But it does mean that when I reflect on my past I can see it in a completely different light. Like the great Renaissance "painters of light," God casts His grace on you, and the picture of your life comes alive.

Have you truly embraced this truth? Have you fully received God's forgiveness for all the sins of your past? And how would you know? Are there still sins of your past that continue to beat you up periodically, or often? Do you keep bringing up sins of your past that God has long since *forgotten*? Or here's a sure sign: Do you have trouble forgiving others? Do you keep bringing up the sins of others and choose not to forgive them? Are you quick to blame and slow to forgive? If so, you have not fully embraced God's grace for which Christ died to give you.

I want to help release you from that kind of life. Too many of us have never truly realized that our past has been rewritten. We are no longer who we were, and we can experience His grace fully! Too many people who have received Christ's forgiveness have remained unkind, rigid, unforgiving, legalistic, religious, bitter, and unwilling to extend grace to others. God wants you to change.

- **I can choose to live *as if* I've never sinned.**

In the Old Testament, the prophet Isaiah shows up at a time when God's people had turned away from Him. The Law had served its purpose and run its course and God's plan for salvation through Christ was coming. Isaiah felt a fresh breeze of grace beginning to blow on the parched religious landscape. A new era was about to begin, and Isaiah starts the prelude to a new song of God's redemptive work in the world. He ushers in this new thing that God is now doing. This community that He will redeem from captivity will still be the community out of which the Savior will come. This song in the desert will become a grand symphony of God's grace culminating in the Christ event – His birth, life, death, and resurrection. Just listen to the sound of joy coming from the redeemed, the forgiven. Isaiah 35:5-7 says, "Then will the eyes of the blind be opened and the ears of the deaf unstopped. Then will the lame leap like a deer, and the mute tongue shout for joy. Water will gush forth in the wilderness and streams in the desert. The burning sand will become a pool, the thirsty ground bubbling springs." Isaiah prophesies of a day when the past will be rewritten.

This is the life to which you are called. Because of God's grace you can release the sins of your past and move ahead in His forgiveness. If you continue to hold on to the sins of your past you'll never fully embrace this forgiveness. He's done all He can, and just as you must choose to receive His forgiveness, you must now choose to live in it every day. Decide every day to live out a new story that God has now begun in you.

- **I can choose to become alive in Christ.**

Romans 6:4 says, "…just as Christ was raised from the dead through the glory of the Father, we too may live a new life." You were once a caterpillar and now you're a butterfly. The Bible describes this shift as moving from death to life. Now that my past has been rewritten I can leave it behind me. It's no longer of any consequence. I don't have to *make things right* or to pay penance for past sins by serving God. My story is being written in such a way that I can now serve God by serving others with all the right motives.

The caterpillar cannot become the butterfly he is meant to be by simply staying the way he is. The same is true with us. The cross of Christ is all about transformation. But here's the key truth that many miss: This new thing He's doing cannot be accomplished by you. It's *His* thing, not yours. The butterfly is just a caterpillar unless he goes through the transformation process. It's why Jesus said, "I tell you the truth, no one can see the kingdom of God unless he is born again" (John 3:3). Like the caterpillar, you must die to yourself, die to being a caterpillar, and release yourself to the beautiful, miraculous process of transformation that only Christ can accomplish. As you give your life over (and over) to Him, you die to an old way of life.

Before we move on from your past, let's acknowledge that your past involves *pasts* of others as well. Simply put, now that you're forgiven you can forgive others. Obviously your willingness to forgive is intrinsically tied to the forgiven life. In fact, Jesus said that we will experience the forgiveness of God in our lives to the degree that we forgive others (Matthew 6:14-15). Perhaps you've had a hard time forgiving someone because you've misunderstood what forgiveness really is. Or like many people I've talked with, you *have* forgiven someone and don't know it. This may sound strange but I've found that it's helpful to understand what forgiveness is *not*.

Forgiveness is not:

1. Forgetting

You cannot forget what others have done against you. Clara Barton, the founder of the American Red Cross in 1881, was known as the "angel of the battlefield." A reporter once slandered her good name with an unkind lie. Years later, when asked if she had any bad feelings against that reporter she replied, "No, I distinctly remember forgetting that." Paul Tillich once defined forgiveness as remembering the past in order that it might be forgotten – a principle that applies to nations as well as individuals. You can't just choose to forget. But as you remember, forgiveness means you've released that person from your need to get even.

2. Reconciling

True reconciliation takes two people. It is possible for an injured party to forgive an offender without reconciliation. For instance, when an abused person forgives, it doesn't mean that he or she necessarily go back to the abuser.

3. Condoning

Forgiveness does not mean that you excuse bad or hurtful behavior. You can forgive and, at the same time, believe that what was done to you was completely wrong. Some think that if they forgive the offender then that person will think that they are condoning what's been done. They may think that, but *you* don't have to. In fact, you can explain, "I forgive you but I do not condone what you have done."

4. Dismissing

Forgiveness involves taking the offense seriously, not passing it off as inconsequential or insignificant. Even God, in His perfect forgiveness, does not dismiss our sin. He faces it head on and, in fact, paid for it.

5. Pardoning

A pardon is more of a legal transaction that releases an offender from the consequences of an action, such as a penalty. Forgiveness is a personal transaction that releases the one offended from the offense but not necessarily the punishment, though in some cases one may feel that forgiveness is not complete until the punishment is removed. But you *can* forgive someone and still insist on a just punishment for the wrong. However, if you can bring yourself to that point of forgiveness you will release that person from the *need* to be punished. Then forgiveness will do its healing power in both you and in the person who wronged you.

If everyone followed the "eye for an eye" principle of justice, observed Gandhi, eventually the whole world would go blind. Forgiveness is the highest form of mature, Christ-like love. "It is not our capacity to think that makes us human, but our capacity to repent and forgive,"[24] noted Phillips Yancey. "Only humans can perform that most unnatural act, which transcends the relentless law of nature."[25] If you are in position to forgive, or need to forgive someone, thank God, because you have been given the opportunity to take your spiritual maturity to a new level.

About 1830 a man named George Wilson killed a government employee who caught him robbing the mail. He was tried and sentenced to be hanged. But President Andrew Jackson sent him a pardon. Wilson did a strange thing. He refused the pardon. No one knew what to do. The case was carried to the Supreme Court. Chief Justice Marshall wrote the court's opinion. "A pardon is a slip of paper, the value of which is determined by the acceptance of the person to be pardoned. If it is refused, it is no pardon. George Wilson must be hanged." And so he was.

Before you move on, perhaps you need to stop and remove the noose of unforgiveness that's around your neck. You must realize that it's strangling the life of grace out of you. You can't fully live forgiven as long as you are unwilling to forgive. Go ahead and die to the past. Die to yourself and your need for justice. But remember, what the caterpillar calls the end, the butterfly calls the beginning. Your future has been redirected.

CHAPTER 18

Your Future Has Been Redirected

W hat's next is now. Your identity has been redefined, your past has been rewritten, and your future has been redirected. The trajectory of your life has changed. Not only are you heaven-bound; *everything* about your life has changed. Peter Drucker, the great business management guru, once said, "The best way to predict the future is to create it." That's another way of saying, don't let the future come to you, move into it with purpose. The Bible says, "Since no man knows the future, who can tell him what is to come?" (Ecclesiastes 8:7). It is true that no man knows the future, but God does. Jeremiah 29:11 says, "For I know the plans I have for you," declares the LORD, "plans to prosper you and not to harm you, plans to give you hope and a future." Notice that He alone knows the plans, and they are not *my* plans but *His* plans.

God's future story for us is revealed as we live for Him – by obeying Him – in the present. God, who is outside of time, speaks to us from eternity. His future for us is spoken into our present. This life is a journey of faith in which He creates our future as we follow Him in the present. Every decision we make is tied to our future, and as you jump into the stream of God's grace, your destiny changes.

- **Your future is redirected. *You have a new destination.***
  You've heard it said that "life is not a destination but a journey." In many respects this is true, but it does make a difference if you

know where you're going. Studies done on kids in impoverished areas have revealed the power of hope for a brighter future. Children with no sense of a better future outside of what they know have little motivation and growth. As I walk with people experiencing depression or despair we often talk about their *future story*. Visualizing a future story that is positive and different from the present brings hope.

Martin Luther King, Jr. said, "We must accept finite disappointment, but never lose infinite hope." If anyone had a future story it was Martin Luther King, Jr. In the end, it was hope in an eternal future that brought hope and passion to his leadership. 2 Corinthians 5:2 says we all "groan, longing to be clothed with our heavenly dwelling..." Life may be a journey but where you're heading matters. If you rest in the grace of Jesus you have hope for life beyond this life. You have a new destination.

- **Your future is secure.** *You have a new promise.*

This future you're stepping into is locked in; it's unchangeable. 2 Corinthians 5:5 says, "Now it is God who has made us for this very purpose and has given us the Spirit as a deposit, guaranteeing what is to come." While life on earth offers many options, eternity offers only two: heaven or hell. Your relationship to God on earth determines your relationship to God in eternity. When you leave the earth your future is locked in, one way or the other. What's next is now. Your eternity is already in motion.

- **Your future is with God's people.** *You have a new family.*

God's big plan for humanity is to create a family. You were created to love God for eternity and to live in His family. Jesus said you're not born into this family; you must be born *again* into this family. Back to the butterfly. The Monarch butterfly only eats the milkweed plant. Because of this focused diet, birds will not eat them. The milkweed makes the Monarch a poisonous snack. These butterflies migrate from as far north as Canada to as far south as Mexico. And they travel together. The Monarch, with its characteristic orange and black coloration, is probably the most recognizable butterfly of all. But did you know there's another species of butterfly that looks almost exactly like the Monarch? If I showed you a picture of a Viceroy butterfly you would mistake it for a Monarch. Unless of course, you're some kind of lepidopterologist (I just had to drop some science on you).

Here's my point. If I'm a Viceroy, you know what I'm going to do? I'm hanging out with the Monarchs so I don't get picked off! If I'm a Viceroy my best friends are the Monarchs. I'm right in the middle of whatever they're up to. In fact, I might even change my diet. The problem with most of us is that we don't have a selective diet. If you feed on the Word of God you're not easily picked off. You may now be a butterfly, but if you're not feeding on God's Word and connected with other believers, watch out, it's open season. Now that you've joined the migration of God's people in the world, change your diet and stay close to others for protection. An accountable life is a protected life.

- **Your future is now.** *You have a new life.*

What's coming is already here. God knows your future. If you want to catch a glimpse of your eternal future, check out Revelation 21. Our future is a place where there is no more crying or pain or mourning or death; the old has passed away. Then, Jesus says, "Behold, I will make everything new!" (vs. 5) Your future has been redirected. Your past has been rewritten. Your identity has been redefined. You really *are* who you think you are because what's next is now.

Section Five

How to Live Forgiven

"Grace must find expression in life, otherwise it is not grace."
Karl Barth

CHAPTER 19

The Gospel is Bigger Than You Think

Let's review where we've been. We've explored the possibility that you and I have a distorted view of ourselves because of a distorted view of God. We looked deep into what really happened on the cross. We've defined grace as an exchange of our inability to measure up to Christ's measure of perfection (that is to say, our sin for His righteousness). We've learned the importance of right thinking if we are to truly redefine ourselves according to this grace. Now, to the most important aspect of this newfound life: how to actually *live* forgiven.

T.S. Eliot said, "The greatest proof of Christianity for others is not how far a man can logically analyze his reasons for believing, but how far in practice he will stake his life on his belief." Next to the "grace awakening" I experienced earlier in my life, the greatest shift I've had as a Christ follower has been the realization that the Gospel is bigger than I was led to believe. Growing up I learned much about how to get into heaven but not much about how to live until I get there. The underlying message was something like *once forgiven you're in; so just hang on until you get to heaven because that's why you were born – to get to heaven. Meanwhile, try to get as many people as you can into heaven with you.* Now, clearly Jesus told us to go and tell others of His grace and bring them along with us. But I think I heard about two million sermons on how to get to heaven and only a few on what to do until we get there. Isn't there more to life than just waiting on heaven? Clearly there is.

I'm certain that this Gospel, this Good News of grace, is bigger than you think. I am certain that if the fullness of the Gospel can be grasped, it will revolutionize the Christian movement as we know it. Many people believe once you're in you're done; you've crossed the finish line. Most of us have understood salvation in terms of Jesus saving us from the punishment of our sin. Again, as I've gone to great lengths to point out in Chapter 11, this is no small thing, but the Gospel is greater still. I'll put it this way: Jesus didn't die to simply save you from the *punishment* of your sin, He died to save you from *your sin*. Here and now. Jesus has something more of a transformation in mind.

When you acknowledge Jesus as the One and Only Forgiver and Lord of your life, *everything* changes. As He becomes the Ruler (Lord) of every aspect of your life, you begin to experience a newfound *freedom* from sin and a grace-filled life of service and love. Your heart breaks over the things that break the heart of God, and you start to see the world in a completely different way. Having lived in bondage you now realize that the only logical response to Christ is to learn to live in this freedom. Surprisingly, most Christians don't.

Harry Houdini, the famed escape artist, issued a challenge wherever he went. He claimed that he could be put in any jail cell in the world and in short order set himself free. Once he went into a jail cell and the doors clanged shut behind him. As was his manner of escape, he then pulled out a concealed piece of metal, strong and flexible, and began to try and pick the lock. He worked feverishly for 30 minutes but no avail. The story goes that after two hours, Harry Houdini collapsed in exhaustion and failure against the door he could not unlock. But when he fell against the door, it swung open! The door had never been locked at all. But in his mind it was locked, and that was all it took to keep him from opening the door and walking out of the jail cell.

Christ came to set us free from bondage. The Bible says, "It is for freedom that Christ has set us free..." (Galatians 5:3). Sounds redundant, doesn't it? But it's not. He came to set us free so that we could live in freedom – live forgiven. He came to restore a broken world and redeem broken people and to set the captives free. Strangely enough, the Bible says we can actually be set free from sin and yet still live in bondage, not realizing the extent to which we've been set free. Only when we stop, give up, and admit our inability to set ourselves free can we escape.

The question I want you to ponder is this: What is the Gospel? And if you have received the Gospel, which "Gospel" have you received? Is it primarily a Gospel of forgiveness, fulfillment, or freedom? This is a critical question to answer if you're going to live this new life. In the end, the answer to the question will get right to the heart of what it means to "live forgiven".

Let me break it down and you decide. I'm grateful to author/pastor, Mark Driscoll, who in his book, *Confessions of a Reformissional Pastor,* has challenged me to think more deeply about this.[24] He notes that different kinds of churches tend to highlight certain aspects of the Gospel. While I appreciate his clarity about different types of churches, (traditional, contemporary, emerging) I dislike the practice of labeling people or groups into neatly defined theological categories. We tend to pigeonhole people and label them along with others without taking time to really listen and discern what they truly believe. I suppose it's easier that way and helps us confirm that what we already believe is right (and it doesn't require *us* to change). Driscoll states that traditional churches tend to preach mostly a Gospel of *forgiveness.*

• The Gospel of Forgiveness

This message goes like this: We have sinned against God and are under His wrath until we ask for forgiveness and choose to repent from our sin. Okay, nothing wrong with that, but Driscoll notes, "This Gospel worked for people in Christendom because they had a general understanding of authority, sin, judgment, hell, and Jesus."[27] Hang with me here; I want to stretch your thinking.

Though this made sense to most people at one time, it is now most often received as "judgmental, mean-spirited, naïve, and narrow-minded to the ever-growing number of people who do not understand the basic tenets of Christianity."[28] I know many Christians who read these words and think, *well, they just need to get with it! That's the Gospel I received, and it does not change. They need to change.* Certainly the Gospel does not change, but *we* can change as we come to greater understanding. This Gospel is not being heard, much less received. Most non-Christians today struggle to make an immediate decision to turn from sin and receive Jesus because they have no framework to know what sin is or who Jesus is. While this had been true of generations past and certain cultures around the world, young people in the West have a particularly distorted view of Christianity in our generation. Most students who hear the Gospel explained this way will look at you like you're from another planet. Which explains, in part, why fewer and fewer are coming to Christ. My concern here is not so much about *how* the Gospel is presented (though that matters), but rather the very essence of the Gospel itself. Here's the greater question I want to ask – is forgiveness alone the sum total of the Gospel?

•   The Gospel of Fulfillment

Driscoll goes on to explain that the contemporary church gener- ally proclaims a Gospel of *fulfillment*. By the way, this is the "Gospel" you hear preached most often on Christian television these days. It must be what people want to hear. I can't watch it; it drives me nuts. In its worst form it's a "name it, claim it" Gospel where God is reduced to a big vending machine in the sky, and we are whining kids demanding whatever goodie we want Him to dispense to us. If He doesn't come through, we either don't have enough faith or He is impotent. I don't find this "gospel" in the Bible. This "Gospel of fulfillment" shows up in our churches in more subtle ways. It finds its way into the church in the form of what I call "pragmatic preaching." Clearly the Bible is meant to be practical and applied into every area of life but in our efforts to show people how to win at work, manage their finances, or raise healthy kids, we may have lost the real Gospel.

Driscoll notes that this gospel of fulfillment is influenced by psychology more than theology. This gospel reflects the psychology of Abraham Maslow and his hierarchy of needs. Of course, Maslow was right that people move from basic survival needs to the higher needs of an "actualized self," seeking to reach their full potential. But underneath Maslow's psychology is this: Ultimately you and I become our own god. Bring this framework over into your spiritual life and you begin to believe that God exists *for me*, not me *for Him*. Don't we seem to hear a lot of this in our churches today? God exists only so that I might maximize my fullest potential. Jesus becomes my ticket to health and wealth or whatever I need Him to be *for me*.

Again, we will never reach our fullest potential in this life apart from Christ, but His death on the cross was not solely for *our* fulfillment. Driscoll explains, "The therapeutic gospel is a false gospel and an enemy of mission for many reasons."[29] It doesn't call me to love God or my neighbor, but instead to love myself. It doesn't call me to God's mission but rather calls Him to my mission. The church doesn't exist to serve God's mission, but instead to help make me a better person. Finally, Driscoll notes, "it takes pride, which Augustine called the mother of all sins, and repackages it as self-esteem, the maidservant of all virtue."

These words resonate with me as I see many people in the church today who are in it for themselves. A consumer mentality is so prevailing that it impacts everything from service times, music styles, children's programs, to what the pastor wears on Sunday mornings. Where else in our culture do strangers send letters to you telling you that they don't like what you're wearing? I once had a guy tell me, "If Jesus were here (at church) He'd be wearing a suit." He had forgotten that Jesus was a homeless man. It seems everything needs to be the way *I* want it to be so that *I* might be *fulfilled* in *my* Christian experience. Again, I don't find this gospel in the Bible.

• The Gospel of Freedom

At its core, the Gospel is one of freedom. This is the Gospel of the apostolic (early) church, and it is the Gospel of the Christ-centered church in our emerging culture. According to the Gospel of freedom we have been made in the image of God and created to live in union with Him and others. Our choice to live for ourselves has wreaked havoc on ourselves and all of creation. We have become enslaved by our sin and the destructive patterns of our self-focused living.

We have a southbound, gravitational pull toward sin and cannot break ourselves free from it. God, in Christ, has come to restore all things back to His original plan and to liberate all of creation from the downward spiral of sin. This, of course, is what Paul meant in Romans 8 when he described all of creation as a mother moaning in childbirth, longing to be set free from this pain, ready to give birth to something new. Verse 21 says, "…the creation itself will be liberated from its bondage to decay and brought into the glorious freedom of the children of God." Jesus came to "liberate" us from bondage and lead us to a "glorious freedom" found in Him alone.

It's worth noting that the word *Christ*, found throughout the New Testament, is the Greek translation for the Hebrew word "Messiah" which means "liberating king." No wonder Peter's declaration, "You are the Christ, the Son of the Living God" (Matthew 16:16), was so monumental. He was more accurate about the purpose of Christ's coming than he realized (until Jesus so clearly affirmed Him). And no wonder when Pilate asked, "Are you the king of the Jews?" Jesus answered without hesitation, "Yes, it is as you say" (Matthew 27:11). He was further establishing the fact that He was the Liberating King. Of course, to say that you are the Liberating King in the Roman Empire at that time was a death wish, especially in a city bearing Caesar's name.

The Gospel of freedom proclaims that Jesus has come to forgive us so that we might be set free and live in freedom. Again, Paul echoes these words in Galatians 5:1, "…it is for freedom that Christ has set us free." Most often we think of this freedom as freedom from sin and yet again, it's bigger than that. It's a freedom that results in the mission of Jesus; namely, we can now join His mission to set others free.

This Gospel of freedom is seen clearly throughout the Bible. The story of Moses and the Exodus (liberation, freedom) is the central story of the Old Testament and remains God's *big* story. Paul adopts his understanding of redemption from the Exodus story. To receive the Gospel means that we are liberated by God through Christ from slavery to freedom. Clearly this is the recurring theme of God's redemptive story throughout history. Is this not the story we find ourselves in today?

This is not some "emerging" expression of the Gospel as much as it is *the* Gospel as it has always been. If the idea of an emerging gospel makes you nervous, fear not, it's simply a rediscovery of what the Gospel has been all along. It's not moving to something new; it's simply discovering our future by rediscovering our past. I see a new generation of (mostly) young church leaders who are willing to die for this Gospel of grace and, at the same time, see its application in our culture as dynamic. If you read the Bible cover to cover it becomes obvious that God has revealed Himself progressively throughout history. The previous discussion regarding Law and grace centers on the fact that God has revealed Himself in His own time and in His own way. Hasn't He revealed Himself progressively to you? Did *He* change or did *you*?

Here's my point: I think our Message *has* changed. I should probably say *we've* changed as we've come to more fully understand the never-changing Message of God. This is why I believe that many Christians *do* need to change their understanding of the Gospel. We must admit that we've not fully embraced the holistic nature of the Gospel. If *you* grow in your understanding of the Gospel shouldn't that result in personal change?

So, what do you say? Is it primarily a Gospel of forgiveness, fulfillment, or freedom? Which Gospel have *you* received? The Gospel is *not* limited to any one of these options. It's bigger still. God's forgiveness is the gateway to fulfillment and freedom. The holistic nature of the Gospel includes all three. We are forgiven, fulfilled, and free in Christ and, "so if the Son sets you free, you will be free indeed" (John 8:36).

All this talk of "different" gospels is simply multiple expressions of the same Gospel. It all points us to the *one* Gospel: the Gospel of Grace. This is no small thing. I believe as the church today reactivates the misplaced Gospel of grace, we'll once again be a part of a world-changing revolution. Forgiveness, fulfillment, and freedom are all intrinsically connected in the life and mission of Jesus. And at the center of it all is Jesus Himself, the Lord of all.

Wherever He is acknowledged as Lord, grace rules the day. This is simply another way of saying, "Jesus is Lord." This was the central declaration of the early church and the central guiding reality for anyone who wants to follow Him. Remember earlier when I said the central focus of Jesus' message was His identity? Well, now *your* identity is found in *His* identity – namely, that He is Messiah, "Lord." As He increasingly becomes Lord of your life, you become more of who you are intended to be. In the few remaining chapters let's explore how you can live in this Gospel of grace as you allow Jesus to reign over all aspects of your life. I think you'll discover that, like God, the Gospel is bigger than you think.

CHAPTER 20

Staying "in Him"

So this Gospel of grace leads to freedom; but freedom from what? Or better yet, freedom *to* what? Let's explore how this *big* Gospel is lived out. In these last three chapters, consider the three major aspects of this life forgiven or what I call the *Jesus life*. We can express our partnership with this God of grace by understanding three simple words: *know*, *grow*, and *show*. You and I exist to *know* Christ, to *grow* in Christ, and to *show* Christ to the world. Now that you're forgiven you are free to *know* Him, and because you are free from sin and self you can actually *grow* to become like Him. This freedom leads you to *show* His love by serving others. These three simple words correspond with the three most important aspects of the Christian life: worship, discipleship, and mission. They find their expression in a life of personal and private *worship*, a life lived *in* and *from community*, and a life *on mission* with Jesus.

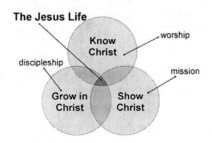

167

As you can see, these three aspects of the *Jesus life* are syner-gistic. That is to say that when combined there's a greater effect than when any singular aspect is absent. In fact, if any one sphere is missing, it is no longer the *Jesus life*. In the remaining chapters we'll look at each sphere, one at a time. In this chapter we'll focus on how to *know* Christ and what it means to *worship* Him. In the next chapter we'll explore what it means to *grow* in Him as we partner with Him to transform us. Then, in the final chapter, we'll see how to *show* His love to our world by living *on mission* with Him.

First, what it means to *know* Him. Earlier in Chapter 13 we noted that 2 Corinthians 5:21 says, "in Him" we have become the righteousness of God. Once you embrace the fullness of this Gospel of freedom, you must determine to live in it, to remain in it. That is, to stay "in Him." Jesus is at once the Origin and Sustainer of this grace, or as Paul puts it in Hebrews 12:2, He is the "Author and Perfecter" of it all. In John 15, Jesus explains that staying "in Him" is to "abide" in Him. He says if we "abide" in Him we will "bear much fruit." Like branches that must stay connected to the vine (the source of life) we are to "remain in" or *live in* Him. The language He uses, to "keep on abiding," suggests a perpetual communion. Of course the challenge with life is that it is, well, so daily. This freedom in Christ must be maintained and sustained, or we'll slip right back into our old way of life. It is clearly a daily struggle to remain in this newfound identity, this newfound freedom, and to live in it. This struggle *is*, in fact, the Christian life.

One of my heroes of faith is Oswald Chambers, a twentieth century Scottish minister best known for his work, *My Utmost for His Highest*. Years ago, while reading this daily devotional guide, I had something of a divine moment. It was the spiritual equivalent of a light bulb coming on, or better yet, a bonfire that started in my heart. On August 4th, the entry reads, "The most important aspect of Christianity is not the work we do, but the relationship we maintain and the surrounding influence and qualities produced by that rela-tionship. That is all God asks us to give our attention to, and it is the one thing that is continually under attack."[30]

Put another way, the key to the Christian life is not found in what you *know* about God or even in what you *do* for God. The key to the Christian life is found in the *intimacy* that we have with God through Christ, and the character and qualities that are produced as a result of that one relationship. I like how Chambers brings it to the point of a spear: That's the *one* thing He's called you to. Then he notes it's the one thing that will be constantly under attack in your life. If you have ever tried to maintain a vibrant, daily walk with Christ, hasn't that been your experience? It has certainly been mine. In fact, as a guy who has been devoted to this kind of life for years, I can tell you that it is a battle. Chambers is right; your intimate pursuit of Christ in this manner will constantly be under attack. Though often private, personal, and quiet, this is a war.

Think of it this way. Your newfound identity in Christ is the result of His forgiveness covering you like a blanket of grace. You are literally "in Him." The Christian life is the constant battle of staying in Him. Salvation comes in a moment, in the midst of a Holy Spirit-led process, and once you receive Christ's forgiveness you're forever saved. But you must remain in that place of grace if you are to truly live forgiven. I could argue that the most important question for the Christ follower is this: How can I stay "in Him"? This question is huge and I cannot overemphasize the importance of the discovery and application of the answer. It becomes the central focus of your life because out of your relationship with Jesus comes everything else. He is, after all, Lord over all.

My friend, Thom, used to coach his son's Little League baseball team. But he didn't just coach the team, he was a kind of psycho-coach (all for the love of his son, mind you). Every year Thom's teams would be virtually unbeatable. He would take the kids on a spring training trip and work out on a field just outside the Texas Rangers ball field. Assuming he recruited the best players (or offered these ten year olds long-term contracts) I asked how they won year after year. He told me that it wasn't that his players were any better than players on other teams. "The difference," he said, "is that I teach the kids how to be *in position* to make the play." He explained that whether the kids were at the plate or in the field, he taught them where to be in that moment, in order to have the highest percentage to make the right play.

This is an apt analogy of the Christian life. If you and I are to remain *in Him* we must put ourselves *in position* to do so. This is at the heart of personal worship. I've discovered this axiom at work in my life: If I put myself in position to hear from God, He speaks; if I don't, He doesn't. Of course the truth is, if I'm in position to listen I hear Him. I've discovered that there is a delicate, if not maddening, balance that must take place in my daily walk with God. It's a kind of spiritual dance with God; though more often like an awkward middle school dance. I often wonder who's leading whom, and I'm not sure I'm quite in rhythm with the song that's being played. Still, I prefer to be on the floor with Him instead of holding up the proverbial wall. The balance is found as I do my part and allow God to do His part (more on that in the next chapter). I'm certain that it is only the Spirit of God that can do this transforming work in me, but at the same time, I know there are certain things that *I* must do if it is to happen.

These things that you and I must do have been known as the "spiritual disciplines." I'll call them spiritual practices. They are spiritual because only God can change us, and they are disciplines because only through our partnering with God can we be transformed. Let me be clear; being transformed means becoming like Jesus. If I am to live forgiven it means that I will live a life that looks like the life of Jesus. But there's a key learning that most Christians have missed.

Years ago, you probably saw a kind of Christian campaign that made its way through the subculture (let's admit that's what it is) of Christianity in America. Perhaps you saw the WWJD armbands and other products. "What would Jesus do?" became the question for many. This is, of course, a great question, but there is a fallacy latent in it pragmatically. The thought that I could, in the moment, decide to do exactly what Jesus would do is not as simple as an armband or acrostic. If you are to make decisions in the moment that would be the same as those Jesus would make, it will happen only as you make these decisions in the context of a life that looks like the life of Jesus. In order to do what Jesus would do you need live like Jesus lived.

This idea begs the question *how did Jesus live?* What did He *do* that put Him in position to make the right decision every time? The answer is found in the continuous intimacy of relationship that He had with the Father. His identity and His mission remained intact as He found Himself before the Father. We see this from the very beginning of His ministry. At Jesus' baptism the Father said, "This is my Son whom I love; with Him I am well pleased." (Matthew 3:17) This is significant because this blessing of affirmation takes place before Jesus had done anything. His identity and His worth was determined by the Father ahead of time, and it was the constant source of encouragement and power throughout His ministry. Jesus found His identity in the Father's love. I've learned that my personal prayer time is most often a moment for me to be reminded again of who (and whose) I am. Often my prayer is "Lord, remind me again of who I am in You. I will allow *You* to define who I am today." This keeps me centered and on mission with Him.

Jesus had certain practices in His life that assured that He would hear from the Father; one being personal prayer. These "practices" were simply expressions of the love relationship He had with His Father. Over and over the Gospel writers tell us that He went away alone to pray. On occasion He prayed all night. Of all the things that the disciples could have asked Him to teach them (how He did that healing thing or how they too could impress their friends and family by walking on water), they asked Him to teach them how to pray like He did.

Can you imagine eavesdropping on a private moment between Jesus and His Father? Imagine no more. It's a good thing the disciples, so curious to see how and what Jesus prayed, listened in for us. What we find over and over in the prayers of Jesus is a radical dependence and raw intimacy with the Father. His primary prayer could be summed up as *Not my will but Yours be done.* This ought to serve as a clue toward our prayers. On one occasion, after Jesus claimed to be equal to the Father, He said "I tell you the truth, the Son can do nothing by Himself; He can do only what He sees His Father doing, because whatever the Father does the Son also does." (John 5:19) This brings incredible insight to us about this Jesus life and how we can live forgiven. Just as Jesus only did what his Father did, we now join Him in His mission in the world. How was it that Jesus could do only what the Father was doing, and how did He know what the Father was up to?

The answer is found in His abiding prayer life. We must live with the same radical dependence and the same pattern of passionate prayer as Jesus did. As desperate prayer-soaked people clinging to Jesus, we can live a life that looks like His life. If Jesus is to be Lord and Ruler of our lives then we must cling to His presence and guidance through a deep, consistent life of prayer.

Let's be honest: Most of us struggle to pray as we should. I think *the* definitive book on prayer and the surrounding spiritual practices is Richard Foster's *Celebration of Discipline*. In it he outlines the "inward disciplines" (meditation, prayer, fasting, and Bible study), the "outward disciplines" (simplicity, solitude, submission, and service), and the "corporate disciplines" (confession, worship, guidance, and celebration) that help keep us in position to stay "in Him." He calls the spiritual disciplines the "door to liberation." He says, "Superficiality is the curse of our age. The doctrine of instant gratification is a primary spiritual problem. The desperate need today is not for a greater number of intelligent people, or gifted people, but for deep people."[31] "Deep people" are those whose roots run to the heart and mind of God.

Here's where the dance comes in. These practices are not religious duties or ways to appease God. We do not practice these disciplines because He has told us to or so He'll be pleased with us. It's quite the other way around. We are so overwhelmed by all that He has done (and is doing) that we cannot help but be drawn to Him. It's His love that compels us. We love Him because He first loved us. Worship is simply our response to God for who He is and what He has done. If you are to live forgiven it will be because you have grasped the extent of His grace and have determined to respond to His grace by giving your life fully to Him. He will now be the reigning King of your life.

"Jesus is Lord." This is the definitive phrase and singular confession of Christian worship. I'm indebted to author, pastor, and leader Alan Hirsch for his insights on this powerful truth. He has noted through his study of Christian movements (including the initial New

Testament movement) that there has always been a white-hot focus on the importance of Jesus. This may seem self-evident, but I think it is a misplaced reality. In his book, *Forgotten Ways*, Hirsch reminds us that from the beginning the one thing that has set the people of God apart is the worship of *one* God.[32] From the start God states that He is the only God, and there is no other. The very first commandment is "You shall have no other gods before me" (Exodus 20:3). He alone is to be worshipped. The *Shema* (the greatest of all commands in the Torah) found in Deuteronomy 6:4-5 says, "Hear, O Israel: The Lord our God, the Lord is one. Love the Lord your God with all your heart and with all your soul and with all your strength." This greatest commandment is prefaced by the singular, guiding truth: God is *one*. In a world of multiple gods, Yahweh shows up and says, "I am." He is the only God; He alone is to be worshipped. This radical monotheism is what set the people of Israel apart. No longer would there be different gods for every sphere of life. The god of the sun, the god of the river, or the god of fertility would all be replaced by the *One* God who rules over all aspects of life. He is Lord, Ruler, and King of all.

Hirsch points out that this radical monotheism shifts when Jesus comes on the scene. The primal confession that "Yahweh is Lord" now becomes "Jesus is Lord." In what he calls a radical "Christocentric monotheism" the Christian finds his or her singular expression of worship: "Jesus is Lord."[33] There is *one* reference point for all of life and existence, and it is Jesus. Paul would say, "...there is one Lord, Jesus Christ, through whom all things came and through whom we live" (1 Corinthians 8:6). Romans 10:9 says, "That if you confess with your mouth, 'Jesus is Lord,' and believe in your heart that God raised Him from the dead, you will be saved." Jesus as Lord over all was the singular confession of the early church and the reason so many were martyred. The early believers refused to see Jesus as merely one of the pantheon of gods in Rome. In this backdrop you can see that the statement "Jesus is Lord" was a deeply subversive claim that completely undermined the rule of Caesar.

It's important to note that the early believers' primary claim was not "Jesus is Savior." Nor do we see that they received Christ as their "Savior" but as "Lord." It is clear that the primary focus in our day is Jesus as Savior and not Lord. I say all this because a personal passion for Jesus as Lord is at the core of worship and as we'll see, the singular focus of discipleship.

A Personal Passion for Jesus

Worship and prayer are core practices because they lead us to, and at the same time bring expression to, a personal passion for Jesus. Anyone who wants to *know* Christ and *grow* in Him will have a passion for Jesus. The primary requirement is a longing after God. Cultivating a passion for Jesus happens as we worship Him. This worship is not primarily a corporate experience but a personal one. Consider that any church-going person might have one or two worship experiences with a larger number of people during a single week. Surely, if that's all worship is, you're *worshipping* God about two out of 168 hours in a week. Sadly, this is the "worship" pattern for many Christians. Clearly this would not describe a passion for Jesus.

You may have noticed in this chapter on worship I have not once mentioned music. It's not because I don't like music. I'm a musician and love all kinds of music. But many people have relegated worship to music. Jesus never said a word about music, but He said much about worship. In fact, He had an uncanny way of simplifying such broad and deep topics as worship. In response to the Pharisees' question about which commandment was greatest, Jesus gives His singular defining statement about worship. Quoting the *Shema*, Jesus said, "Love the Lord your God with all your heart and with all your soul and with all your mind. This is the first and greatest commandment. And the second is like it: Love your neighbor as yourself. All the Law and the Prophets hang on these two commandments" (Matthew 22:37-40). Jesus says we are to love God comprehensively. This is worship. He says nothing about a corporate gathering of people singing and listening to someone speak, which again is what most Christians have relegated their *worship* to be. Corporate worship is very important but not as important as private worship. In the end, Jesus is saying that worship is life itself.

We must explore one more aspect of Christian worship. If a *passion for Jesus* is at the core of worship then the *Kingdom of God* is the result or outcome of worship. As noted, personal worship begins with personal prayer. It should be freeing to know that there are many ways to pray personally, but as we will see, if at some point our prayers do not lead to action, they are meaningless. Prayer is where the Kingdom life (again, the *Jesus life*) begins. I confess through much of my life and ministry my prayers have been focused on me. My prayer life came alive when I realized that prayer has little to do with my needs and more to do with aligning my life with the Kingdom – the will of God.

This is huge. Jesus taught us to pray, "Your Kingdom come, Your will be done, on earth as it is in heaven" (Matthew 6:10). The great focus of prayer is the will of the Father. Could it be for years your prayers have been focused on you? Could it be that my prayers have been all about my needs, my wants, my life, my family, my job, *my kingdom*? The reality is prayer has very little to do with what *I* want and everything to do with what *God* wants. Could it be that we've been praying for *our* kingdom to come and not *His,* and could this be why we've been so frustrated in prayer?

Consider again the Lord's Prayer. Here's when the light came on for me. I realized that there is only one line out of ten that focuses on my needs. One tenth or ten percent of a model prayer from Jesus has to do with *me*. If *my* needs were actually a smaller part of my prayers and I focused more on the other ninety percent (which is what prayer is really about), then the other ten percent makes sense and comes alive.

When Jesus does show us how to focus on our needs it becomes even more sobering. In the Lord's Prayer, a model on how we should pray, we see that the *one* line about *me* is actually about my needs and not my wants. And even then, it's about my *daily* needs. God simply wants me to focus on life with Him today. He wants to give me enough for the day. It's why Jesus would tell us not to give a lot of thought to tomorrow or be anxious about tomorrow. Just focus on today. He promised to take care of us today. (Matthew 6:25-34)

Notice that a personal passion for Jesus involves a passion for His Kingdom. The content of our prayers is for His Kingdom to come, "on earth as it is in heaven" (Matthew 6:10). Why would God want our prayers to be Kingdom-focused? Because that's where

He wants us to live. That's what our lives are all about. Forgiven people are Kingdom people. How do you think His will is being accomplished in Heaven right now? Perfectly. Every day in Heaven God's will is being accomplished perfectly. Think about this: There is no sin, no rebellion, no suffering, no one is abandoned, no one is unforgiven. There is no injustice, there is no prejudice, there are no orphans, no one is seen as *less than* someone else by virtue of their intelligence, the color of their skin, their appearance, their political persuasion, or the country from which they come. The slave and the king are the same, and that's what He wants on earth, *now*.

Having a passion for Jesus, then, requires a shift from my will to God's will. Is your heart's desire for His will to be done, for His Kingdom to show up wherever you go? Instead of asking, "What's God's will for my life?" simply ask, "What's God's will?" Could it be that the content of your prayers would change from a focus on you and yours and become predominantly about the Kingdom of God and not about *your* kingdom? This is at the heart of worship, and it will revolutionize your prayer life.

While formerly you may have prayed for God to help you with your finances, you would now practice restraint in your spending. Instead of bringing no spiritual thought to your finances, you would determine to consult God for guidance while actually making a purchase. Your prayers would shift from, *God, you've got to allow me to get this house* to, *Lord, I'd like to allow you to be Lord of my home.* Instead of, *God, you've got to help me save this relationship* (which usually means, *God, please change that person*), you would actually pray, *Lord, change me.*

A passion for Jesus and His Kingdom are at the heart of worship. "But seek first the Kingdom of God and His righteousness and all these things will be given to you as well" (Matthew 6:33). After all the angst over worship styles, music preferences, and all we've made worship out to be, in the end it is one person coming before God saying *Not my will but Yours be done.* Until we've come to that point we have not worshipped God. In the end worship is surrender. I will now choose to partner with God as He takes over my life.

CHAPTER 21

Partnering with God

ᘿᕈ

If you want to live forgiven you must *know* Christ, *grow* in Christ, and *show* Christ to the world. Let's turn our attention to the *grow* aspect of the Jesus life. Growing in Christ corresponds with discipleship, but because the word has become so convoluted, I like to speak of discipleship as life *in* and *from* community. Discipleship is understood by most as *learning,* which implies classrooms and teachers. Many people think that if they're learning more they're becoming more like Jesus. Sadly, some of the most biblically knowledgeable people I've known have been among those most unlike Christ. Clearly there are things we must know in order to be disciples of Jesus, but if our goal is to grow to become like Him, we don't need more information about Jesus, we need more of Jesus Himself. He didn't tell us to follow after more information or knowledge. He said, "Follow *me.*"

If you have a passion for Jesus, then partnering with Him to become more like Him will become the joy of your life. Because we follow a God of grace, our motivation is not a *religious* motivation. It seems we always lean toward religion and not relationship with Christ. If we've embraced the grace of Jesus there is a newfound motivation for obedience. Several years ago, I heard pastor and author Erwin McManus reference Psalm 119:32.[34] It says, "I run in the path of your commands for you have set my heart free." McManus noted that most people in our world, including many Christians, would never think of *commands* and *freedom* in the same sentence. Most of us think of commands as being confining and restricting, not liberating and freeing. Freedom comes as we run *in* the path of His commands, not *away* from them. As you decide to follow God's commands you realize that you've just stepped into a place not of seclusion or confinement, but a place of wide open spaces. In His commands is where I find freedom, because freedom is not found in doing whatever I *want* to do but in doing what I *ought* to do. Given over to what *I* want to do has not fared so well for me.

In the previous chapter we talked much about personal prayer and worship. As we continue to consider how to grow into Christ-likeness, a few more practices must become a central part of our lives. These practices were at the core of life in the early church. A personal passion for Jesus as Lord is followed by a commitment to "covenant life together," a radical engagement with Scripture, and a dedication to personal transformation. Let's unpack these core practices.

Covenant Life Together

A covenant life together with other believers is at the heart of living forgiven. We are saved *from* sin and *to* community and a new way of life. God's great dream for us is to live in community together. Becoming more like Jesus will not happen apart from the family of God because the Spirit of God uses the Word of God in the context of the family of God to help us become like the Son of God. The early church modeled this critical practice through a web of smaller missional communities. It wasn't that they had a nicely formed "small group strategy." They had simply decided that Jesus would be Lord. They joined in covenant relationships with one another so that together they could allow Him to be Lord. Recognizing that we all connect and experience relationships in different ways our church has made a radical commitment to doing life together in groups. Some are large, some mid-size, and some are small. We agree that a *life-on-life* kind of covenant takes place best in smaller groups. All of our groups:

- Foster a culture of belonging and acceptance
- Facilitate a Spirit-led journey toward Christ through constant learning
- Focus on missional living by engaging their community and their world
- Flourish through innovative and flexible forms and structures
- Follow a process of releasing members to reproduce groups and new believers in Christ

The heartbeat of every group is a passionate devotion to Jesus as Lord and a radical commitment to His Kingdom coming to earth through us. As we join Jesus together we become entrenched in one another's lives and experience what the Bible calls *koinonia*, true fellowship. As He reigns in us, wherever we go His Kingdom shows up.

Engagement with Scripture

The integration of Scripture into life is foundational for every Christ follower. We've noted that growing more like Jesus is not about information but transformation. A commitment to personal transformation is the pathway to spiritual growth and a clearer understanding of the Scriptures. But knowledge of the Scriptures is of little help if we do not practice what it says. We must approach the Scriptures with the primary objective of being transformed, not informed. I've learned that the more a person is devoted to the authority of Scripture the more apt they are to want to learn more. In "church-speak" we want to *go deeper*. The problem is that the more people grow in knowledge alone, the more they want to use that knowledge over others. Many Christians tend to argue over the truth and interpretation of Scripture rather than focus on the application of Scripture. They've gone the way of the Pharisees, believing that the Bible is a set of rules to be followed, rather than the alive, active, and transformational Word of God. In John 5:39-40, Jesus said, "You diligently study the Scriptures because you think that by them you possess eternal life. These are the Scriptures that testify about me, yet you refuse to come to me to have life." Personal transformation is activated when you *do* what the Bible says in the context of a personal passion for Jesus as Lord.

Personal Transformation

If I desire for Jesus to be Lord of my life then I will be devoted to personal transformation. I must realize that personal change is *my* responsibility. This is why I'll commit to live in covenant community with other believers and allow the Bible to be my guide. I will partner with God so that I can become like Jesus. This is personal discipleship. God's love for me has set off a chain of events, as it were. His love results in my love for Him, and now I passionately pursue a life *in Him.*

As I cling to "the Vine," He produces the "fruit" that becomes evidence of His life in me. What is the end result of all of this? Ultimately it's the life of Jesus. I become *Jesus with skin on,* His hands and feet in the world. No wonder He calls His Church (real people living real lives) the "Body of Christ." As I partner with Christ I live out the qualities, the character, and the very heart of Jesus in my world.

What would this look like? Again the Bible doesn't leave us hanging. There are certain inward qualities that find their expression in life. In Galatians 5:22-23, we find what is called "the fruit of the Spirit." Notice it's called the fruit of "the Spirit" not the fruit of "the religious life," the "fruit of the flesh," or the fruit of "one who really works hard for God." No, this fruit is the result of the Spirit's overflowing work. Here's what it says: "But the fruit of the Spirit is love, joy, peace, patience, kindness, goodness, faithfulness, gentleness, and self-control. Against such things there is no law." As you stay in Him, His life is formed in you. The Jesus life expresses itself in acts of grace. To live forgiven means that grace will be the driving expression of my life.

I call this fruit the *nine flavors of grace.* Let's break it down. Love is grace defined. Joy is grace from the inside out. Peace is grace at ease. Patience is grace in waiting. Kindness is grace in the small stuff. Goodness is grace to the core. Faithfulness is grace to the end. Gentleness is the touch of grace. Self-control is grace applied. The fruit of the Spirit becomes a kind of litmus test for the indwelling Spirit of God.

What follows this list of the "fruit of the Spirit" is equally important. "Those who belong to Christ Jesus have crucified the sinful nature with its passions and desires. Since we live by the Spirit, let us keep in step with the Spirit." (Galatians 5:24-25) As you commit your life to Jesus as Lord, these spiritual practices will allow you to remain in Him, and you'll then be walking in step with Jesus.

CHAPTER 22

Living the Mission of Jesus

I heard Rick Warren, pastor and author of The Purpose Driven Life, say something I'll never forget. In his simple yet profound manner he said, "The Body of Christ has had its hands and feet amputated and all that's left is a big mouth."[35] His words brought clarity to what I had been feeling for a long time. How did we come to this? And how could anyone amputate their *own* limbs?

In seminary I learned about the "social gospel," a movement most prominent in the late 19th and early 20th Centuries. The idea was to apply Christian principles to social problems, primarily hunger and poverty. I was told it was a distinctly liberal movement both politically and theologically. I don't know much about what motivated the leaders of that movement or where they stood politically or theologically, but I remember thinking even then when was the Gospel *not* social? I was taught there were two gospels as it were. One was the biblical gospel that had to do with heaven and hell and the glory of God and such. It was best expressed in John 3:16. The other gospel had to do with earth and sin and man and all the mess that comes with that. I was taught much about how to engage myself in the former and very little about the latter. Again, I've discovered that the Gospel is much bigger than I thought.

If anyone was a proponent of the social gospel it was Jesus. As you read the Gospels you discover that no one has ever been more *social* than Jesus. He never ministered at arm's length. This incarnational Savior came as close as possible into our pain, our disease, our sin, and our death. If I am to live the Jesus life I will love God comprehensively and love others as much as I love myself.

As I live forgiven I will seek to *know* Christ through a personal passion for Him. I will *grow* to become like Him through covenant relationships, engagement with the Scriptures, and personal trans-formation. Finally, I will *show* Christ to the world around me as I live on mission with Him. The last of these three simple words brings ultimate expression to this forgiven life.

The Missional Life

A radical devotion to the mission of Jesus is the singular prac-tice that integrates the other spheres of the Jesus life. If you have a passion for Jesus you'll care about the things He cares about, and you'll hate the things He hates. You will devote yourself to cove-nant relationships because you cannot serve the mission of Jesus alone. You commit yourself to the engagement of the Scriptures because it is in them that you are drawn to the mission of Jesus. You are committed to personal transformation because a transformed life overflows into the mission of Jesus in the world. This is the missional life.

Missional is simply an adjective describing a person or group on mission with Jesus, the Primary Missionary. Closely tied to missional living is incarnational living. In fact, you can't have one without the other. If you are to live the mission of Jesus you must do so *in the flesh*. That is to say *in person*. The incarnational life is always up close and personal.

Several years ago I preached a sermon on a Sunday morning about the Good Samaritan. I challenged our people to really see the homeless and the hungry in our area and to allow their lives to be interrupted by their needs. That night as the crowd was arriving for our evening service, I was roaming around outside the church, dressed up like a homeless man. My hair was long and matted and my clothes were torn and dirty. I watched from across the street as the cars filed into the parking lot. I got a sense of what it felt like to be homeless, or at least what it's like to be on the outside looking in. It was strange to see all these "church people" hurrying past to get into the church. Just when I thought no one was going to even recognize me, two teenage girls (scared to death) came over and invited me in. As they got closer I revealed who I was. "Oh, my gosh!" one of them exclaimed. We laughed as I thanked them for being so sweet, so courageous. I told them I was coming in shortly.

Before the opening music was finished, I made my way in and sat down in the middle of the Worship Center. As the normal preaching moment came no speaker was seen. I slowly stood up and walked to the front. I stayed in character as I told of my life as a homeless man and of the need for people who love Jesus to reach out to people like me. By the end of my short message *almost* everyone had figured out who I was. When I was finished I walked out the back, straight to my car, and I drove home. Later one man told another, "That guy was good, but I missed my pastor."

It was interesting, if not troubling, that only two frightened teenage girls came out to speak to me and invite me to join them. I was *not* surprised that it was teenagers who made the effort, but it caused me to wonder why so many others simply passed me by, especially with a sermon on the homeless fresh on their minds. It was either a lesson on the effectiveness of my preaching or on the disconnect between the Bible and life.

When Jesus said that the greatest commandment was to love God comprehensively He added, "…and 'Love your neighbor as yourself.'" (Luke 10:27) When asked *Who is my neighbor?* He went on to tell the story of the "Good Samaritan." The historical context for this story is one of racism, hatred, and oppression. The lawyer's question is our question. Jesus crafts a story so beautifully that it becomes a model for missional life. Check out Luke 10:25-37.

We live missional-incarnational lives when:

- ### We see their faces.
  Have you ever tried *not* to make eye contact with a beggar? I'm ashamed to say that I have. Have you ever heard of the needs of others across the ocean or across town and have hoped that someone would do something? Luke 10:33 says the Samaritan really *saw* the man in distress. He didn't just look at him, he *saw* him. People were

not just a blur in the life of this man. Look into someone's eyes today and see their need.

- **We know their stories.**

The Good Samaritan not only saw the man, he determined to know what had happened to him. It was obvious this man was in need of help. Though sometimes hard to see, we live among needy people. Behind every face is a story, often one of pain, fear, and brokenness. Pick someone in your life and determine to learn their story.

- **We step into their stories.**

The Good Samaritan inconvenienced himself. He was heading somewhere; he had an agenda. Helping people is never convenient. It's much easier to stay to yourself and your own set of problems. A life on mission is interrupted any time we see God on the move. Choose to be interrupted and step into someone's life today.

- **We ease their pain.**

As Jesus tells this story of the Good Samaritan He goes into great detail about how he helped the man in need. You would think that when the Samaritan stops to help the story is over and the point is made. But Jesus wants us to see that caring for others is very specific. You never help people in general terms. You help in very specific ways.

- **We end their search.**

When we stop to see people, learn their stories, step into their lives, and ease their pain, we end their search for help. When they experience the touch of Jesus through our hands and our feet they find what they are looking for. The search for help ends when Jesus is found. As we serve others we lead them to the great Helper. In so doing, we align our life's mission with the mission of Jesus.

In the same way that Jesus knew His mission and aligned Himself to it, every believer and every church that seeks to be missional will be aligned with Jesus' mission. A missional church aligns all of its activities, processes, and resources around the redemptive mission of God. In order for most people and churches to truly become missional, several major shifts must take place. Both individually and corporately these shifts are not easy.

For many of us the individual shift starts as we confess that we've not been living on mission with Jesus. Perhaps while reading this book you've realized that you never really have embraced the totality of the Gospel. There must come a moment of reckoning. It came for me. Through tears I confessed, "Lord, I'm sorry that I've not grasped the fullness of your grace and its impact on my life. The Gospel is much bigger than I realized and I've only been living part of it." If you truly want to live forgiven there must come a moment of repentance.

Repentance will result in several seismic shifts in our lives. We will have to think in new ways about ourselves and our engagement in the mission of God in the world. Throughout the book we've explored several of these personal shifts. The missional life requires a shift from *religion to relationship*. My personal passion for Jesus will guide everything I do. As I live forgiven I will shift from *the past to the present*. As I celebrate what God has done for me in the past, the stories I tell are of what He's doing in me in the present. If I choose to live on mission with Jesus I will shift from *self to servant*. My reference point for decision-making and involvement will shift from *individual to communal* as I bring myself into covenant relationships. My role in the local church shifts from *member to disciple* because I recognize that my personal growth is not the church's job but mine. As I seek to live incarnationally the big shift is from *my life* to *the Jesus life*.

If our churches are to become missional communities, several corporate shifts must take place as well. A new understanding of the mission of God in the world leads us to the first seismic shift: from *church* to *movement*. As we embrace the mission of God as a movement, we will shift from *institution* to *revolution* because we have seen that all of the great Jesus movements take place when God's people have little of what would be recognized as institutional structure and organization. The Church that Jesus envisioned was not an institution but a movement. We will determine to shift from *attractional* to *incarnational*, moving away from a "come and see" to a "go and be" ecclesiology. Starting at home, missional churches move from *local* to *global* as they embrace the worldwide mission of Jesus as their own. As people consider their involvement in God's redemptive work they will shift from *ministry* to *mission*. Ministry is typically seen as a church-related activity while mission is a 24/7 partnership with God.

Church leaders will shift from *control* to *release* as a hierarchy of leadership becomes an apostolic model of shared leadership. The top-down pastoral leadership model, which resembles an American CEO model more than a biblical one, will be replaced with an empowering of all people. Structures and processes will move from *complex* to *simple* as a white-hot focus is brought to mission. Even church buildings will reflect the mission of God as we shift from *extravagance* to *minimal*, desiring to leverage our resources toward others.

Bible teachers will function more as facilitators whose focus will shift from *information* to *transformation*. Teachers will realize personal change takes place through the inhabitation of the Spirit and not simply through more information. Pastors and leaders will shift from *denomination* to *Kingdom* as they embrace the coming of God's Kingdom and the unity in the Body as the prayers of Jesus. In the end we'll shift from *us* to *others*.

Staying on Course

の少

As part of a local multi-sport group, I train with some of my best friends, though my favorite partner is my daughter, Whitney. One of my good friends, Jon Poe, is an Ironman triathlete. You can guess that these people aren't normal. To compete in the Ironman you must swim 2.4 miles, bike 112 miles, and then run a marathon (26.2 miles) to the finish line. Now that's a race. I think I'll stick to sprint and Olympic distances. Not long ago I talked to another friend, Lynn Ballard. He's one of those ultra-marathon runners. He does these 100 mile races. 100 miles... at one time! There's a 30-hour limit and Lynn did it in 23. That's perseverance – or insanity.

As you commit to live forgiven I pray that you will stay on course. Paul wrote to a group of missional people in Thessalonica and said, "We continually remember before our God and Father your work produced by faith, your labor prompted by love, and your endurance inspired by the hope in our Lord Jesus Christ" (1 Thessalonians 1:3). Check out a kind of missional triad that described these people. Their lives were marked by an active faith, grace on display, and an enduring passion for Jesus. What set them apart was not what they believed but what they did. Note the active words used by Paul: work, labor, and endurance. What do you want to be remembered for? You're well aware that many people start out strong but few finish strong. It's how you finish that matters.

While competing in a triathlon in Boulder, Colorado, last summer I met a hero of mine.[36] I had read about Sister Madonna Buder and had seen her on television at the Ford Ironman Triathlon in Kona, Hawaii – the granddaddy of triathlons. Sister Buder is a 20-time Ironman finisher. But catch this: Not only is she a nun, she's also 78 years old. Talk about perseverance. I met her the day before the race in Boulder where she competed in one of the hardest Olympic distance triathlons there is. I got my picture with her, and I look as giddy as a little schoolgirl at a Hannah Montana concert. I was so excited to meet her because I had been so inspired by her persevering life. Sister Buder has been an ambassador for the sport she loves and the Savior she worships.

These examples of perseverance inspire us, not just in sports but in life. Would you describe yourself as a persevering person? Are you determined to run this race of life with perseverance? Maybe you did at one time. Perhaps you've given up. If so, I can bet that you've forgotten that what's next is now. You can finish this race because in all the ways that matter, you already have.

Hebrews 12:1 says that life with God is a race that takes perseverance. In Hebrews 12:1 Paul said, "… let us throw off everything that hinders and the sin that so easily entangles, and let us run with perseverance the race marked out for us." You are at some point along this race that has been marked off for you. And here's the thing – you've got to run your own race and there are no shortcuts.

If you choose to live a life defined by grace, you'll be tempted to take some shortcuts. On April 21, 1980, 23-year-old Rosie Ruiz was the first woman to cross the finish line at the Boston Marathon. She did it in the third-fastest time ever recorded for a female runner – two hours, 31 minutes, 56 seconds. Quite the victory considering she was hardly sweating when crowned with the winner's wreath. Marathon organizers were immediately suspicious after she sprinted across the finish line. After some investigation, course officials had no evidence of Ruiz passing checkpoints. Fellow competitors had no recollection of her.

Eventually a few spectators came forward and said they saw Ruiz join the race during its final half-mile. What makes Ruiz an even bigger cheater is that she also deceived race officials in the New York Marathon, the race she used to qualify for the Boston event. Apparently she got her above-average time by riding the

Manhattan subway! If you are to run the race of a life forgiven you must determine to live this Jesus life from start to finish.

Sadly, like Rosie Ruiz, some of us want to cheat our way to a full and meaningful life. Many never pursue God's finish line, and still others start out strong but they don't finish strong. Galatians 5:7 says, "You were running a good race. Who cut in on you and kept you from obeying the truth?" It's possible to lose your way. Many give up altogether. I know many Christians who are no closer to a grace-filled life than they were ten or twenty years ago. At some point along the way they stopped running. And the moment you stop running the amazing grace race, you stop running the race God intended for you.

Since the start of this journey together I've prayed that you would discover the life that you're meant to live. I pray that you have come alive to the grace of God. As you've discovered how big this Gospel is, I hope you have determined to live in it. Howard Washington Thurman said, "Don't ask yourself what the world needs, ask yourself what makes you come alive. And then go and do that. Because what the world needs is people who have come alive." Nothing brings life like the forgiveness of God. Have you come alive to His grace? Live forgiven.

End Notes

Acknowledgements
1. Max DePree, *Leadership is an Art* (New York: Dell Publishing, 1998), p. 11.

Introduction
2. Philip Yancey, *What's So Amazing About Grace?* (Grand Rapids, MI: Zondervan Publishing House, 1997), p. 11.

3. Robert McGee, *The Search for Significance* (Houston, TX: Rapha Publishing, 1985). I'm personally indebted to McGee for his research and careful attention to Scripture applied to counseling and personal identity. I read his classic book at a critical time in my life. The truths found in it became life changing for me.

Section One
4. John Milton, *Paradise Lost* (New York: New American Library, 1961), p. 160.

5. Yancey, *Rumors* (Grand Rapids, MI: Zondervan Publishing House, 2003), p. 34.

6. C.S. Lewis, *Mere Christianity* (New York: Macmillan, 1968), p.105.

7. For roller coaster aficionados: In case you were wondering, Travis' favorite roller coaster is *Montu* at Busch Gardens in Tampa, Florida, one of the longest and highest inverted roller coasters in the world. The highest drop we've experienced is the first drop on the *Titan* at Six Flags Over Texas in Arlington, Texas. It drops 255 feet at 85 miles per hour. Pretty cool.

8. McGee, chapters 6 and 7.

9. A.W. Tozer, *The Knowledge of the Holy* (New York: NY, Harper Collins Publishers, 1961), p. 1.

10. Jeffrey Kluger, *The God Gene,* (Time magazine, October 25, 2004), p.62.

11. Yancey, *Rumors*, p. 24.

Section Two
12. For more on The Barna Group and the research found there, go to www.barna.org.

13. Dallas Willard, *Renovation of the Heart,* (Colorado Springs: CO, NavPress, 2002), p.22.

14. This story is told by Philip Yancey in *What's So amazing About Grace?,* p. 45.

Section Three
15. Jim Henderson and Matt Casper, *Jim and Casper Go to Church* (Carol Stream: IL, Tyndale House Publishers, 2007).

16. Yancey, *What's So Amazing About Grace?*, p. 59.

17. Watchman Nee, *The Normal Christian Life* (first published in Bombay, India by Gospel Literature Service, 1957), American

edition published in Carol Stream, IL, Tyndale House Publishers, 1977), p. 11.

18. Chris Anderson, *Wired Magazine* article, (August 2003).

Section Four
19. <u>René Descartes</u>, *Discourse on the Method of Rightly Conducting the Reason, and Searching for Truth in the Sciences* (originally published in 1637).

20. Eugene Peterson, *Perseverance: A Long Obedience in the Same Direction* (Downers Grove: IL, InterVarsity Press, 1996).

21. At the time of this writing Taylor was still living in Russia but feel free to ask to see pics of my new nephew.

22. As noted, I'm indebted to Robert McGee and his work, *The Search for Significance*. Read his book for greater understanding of some of these and other passages that speak into the truth of who you have become in Christ.

23. Paul Tillich, *The Eternal Now* (New York: NY, Charles Scribner's Sons, 1963), Chapter 2.

24. Quoted in *What's So Amazing About Grace?*, p.126.

25. Ibid., p.98.

Section Five
26. Mark Driscoll, *Confessions of Reformissional Pastor* (Grand Rapids: MI, Zondervan Publishing House, 2006).

27. Ibid., p. 23.

28. Ibid., 24.

29. Ibid.

30. Oswald Chambers, *My Utmost for His Highest*, special updated version, edited by James Reimann (Grand Rapids, MI: Discovery House Publishers, 1995), August 4th.

31. Richard Foster, *The Celebration of Discipline* (San Francisco, CA: Harper Collins Publishing, 1978).

32. Alan Hirsch, *The Forgotten Ways- Reactivating the Missional Church* (Grand Rapids: MI, Brazos Press, 2006).

33. Ibid., Chapter 3.

34. Erwin McManus, from a message entitled, *The Barbarian Way* at The Leadership Summit, Willow Creek Community Church, 2004?.

35. Rick Warren, from a message at the *Catalyst Conference*, Atlanta, GA, 2007.

36. For more on the coolest Olympic distance triathlon on the planet, go to www.5430sports.com.

Printed in the United States
119859LV00001B/151-1650/P

9 781606 474860